KEYS
FOR
US

CRISTIE
PENN

KEYS FOR US

CRISTIE PENN

DISCOVERING MASCULINE
AND FEMININE IDENTITY, GOD'S WAY

Keys for Us: Discovering Masculine & Feminine Identity, God's Way
Copyright © 2025 Cristie Penn

Published by Keys of Truth, LLC

Cover design: Mallard Agency
Cover author photo: Matthew Yarnell @yarnell.xyz

Paperback ISBN: 979-8-9933225-0-6
eBook ISBN: 979-8-9933225-1-3
Audiobook ISBN: 979-8-9933225-2-0

First Edition: November 2025

CONTENTS

Praise for *Keys for Us* vii

Introduction xv

1. How Two People Who Care About Each Other
   Can Drift Apart 1

2. What's Happened to Our Hearts? 11

3. Different by Design 19

4. Different for a Purpose 33

5. Key #1 For Men: Captivate 43

6. Key #2 For Men: Cultivate 53

7. Key #3 For Men: Communicate 61

8. Key #1 For Women: Captivate 81

9. Key #2 For Women: Cultivate 91

10. Key #3 For Women: Communicate 105

11. In Need of Rescue 125

12. In Position for Reset 135

13. From Learning to Legacy 145

Discussion Questions 155

Acknowledgments 213

About the Author 215

Notes 217

PRAISE FOR *KEYS FOR US*

"My wife and I have been doing marriage counseling for the last 17 years, and the material in this book will definitely become a major part of our counseling going forward. Cristie has truly unlocked the truth about men and women. Everyone interested in having a significant covenant relationship with his or her spouse will love this book."

JIM PACK
Founder and President of One Heart Ministry
Executive Pastor, City Life Church
Dallas/Fort Worth, Texas

"Cristie Penn's desire to see honor restored between men and women shines through. This book attends to building successful relationships, and she has drawn a picture of how men and women can 'dance,' work, love, protect, collaborate and thrive together. In bringing her insight and understanding, she encourages the body of Christ in the practical keys of living in dignity, wisdom, and grace while partnering with one another."

BARBARA BYERS, PHD, LPC
Dallas/Fort Worth, Texas

"What a breath of fresh air this book is. In a time when the world around us seems lost in confusion in relation to gender roles, this book brings clarity and hope. The keys are easy to read, easy to understand, and easy to apply to our lives."

STEVEN KAYLOR
Lead Pastor, Hope Church
Tokyo, Japan

"I first heard snippets of this message on the other side of the world while serving orphans with Cristie Penn in Zambia, Africa. My husband and I were struggling through some marriage issues, and Cristie spoke life to us. God has entrusted a powerful message to this mighty woman of God!"

TAMMIE HEAD
Bible Teacher and Author of *More and Duty or Delight?*

"Hopeful and empowered. That's how you'll feel when you spend time reading this book. If you take to heart these truths and use them—even some of them—your marriage, friendships, and even work relationships will be transformed. I commend Cristie for being authentic enough to listen to the Lord and then translate what she's learned onto paper for all of our benefit!"

LISA ROSE
Founder of First Friday, and Founder and President of Gatehouse
Dallas/Fort Worth, Texas

"This is a Holy Spirit–inspired lesson that will enlighten you, challenge you, and change you. Read it knowing it's not too late to change. I'm thankful Cristie was obedient and allowed the Lord to use her to share truths that will help and heal. The lifechanging keys in this book are straight out of God's Word."

GARY RANDLE
Co-founder/President of the Board, HOPE Farm
Fort Worth, Texas

"As a product of an unsuccessful marriage and two relationships, these truths about men and women have given me stable, Christian-based guidance on how to understand a man. It has also shown me the art of maneuvering around my insecurities with men. The keys have mesmerized me. I've read it over and over and each time a new enlightenment is revealed. I cannot put it down and want to keep it near me for quick reference. It's a must read for every woman looking to have a successful and loving relationship, a manual for every marriage! Cristie was God-inspired to reach women of all ages and backgrounds with words of encouragement for a better life. It has certainly moved and touched my soul, and I look forward to the day God gives me another opportunity to use what I've learned."

EILEEN SALAZAR-SZEP
Senior Executive Administrator to President & CEO,
Royal Caribbean International

"Passionate, determined, beautiful, humble, and full of compassion is how I would describe Cristie. I am not surprised about her desire to obey God's calling to write this book. It offers powerful insight to people who are married, single, and engaged and those who are seeking a relationship according to God's original design. This is an opportunity to rediscover and reposition your heart to unveil and reveal redemptive and practical truths about yourself and the majesty of God's love to restore and heal relationships."

DOROTHY NEWTON
Speaker and Author of *Silent Cry*

"Cristie's book was gifted to me at a time when I was wrestling with emotions I could not understand or articulate. They were causing extreme internal and external conflict! The message was so easy to read, and the personal experiences Cristie authentically shares helped bring clarity to my chaos! As a result of reading and applying what I learned, I now enjoy living with emotional integrity and healed relationships that were once conflicted."

TRACI HORTON
Gospel Music Association Business Advisory Committee Member

"As a Senior Pastor for over 25 years, I've had the privilege of assisting many couples as they navigate the challenges in their relationships.

This book serves as a guiding light for them, clearly defining God's intended design for both men and women. The easily understandable "keys" help couples recognize and appreciate their differences, turning potential points of conflict into sources of celebration. I find great joy in recommending this book, confident that it will foster greater self-awareness and strengthen their relationships."

PASTOR MIKE BANAS
Associate Pastor Milestone Church

"By tapping into God's original design for both genders, we have gained a greater understanding of the needs, desires, and communication styles our Creator hard-wired into the male and female soul. We have learned to both embrace and celebrate our design differences, and while we certainly developed a better understanding of the opposite sex, we may have discovered even more about ourselves along the way. We are so grateful for the tremendous impact this book continues to have in our lives!"

DAVID AND BRITTANY DANCER

"My eyes have opened to the role God designed for me from a deeply biblical perspective. Cristie Penn's approach isn't just personal—it's rooted in Scripture. She unpacks how God created both men and women with purpose, and how understanding that divine design brings freedom, not limitation. Her story helped me see that embracing my God-given role isn't about fitting into a mold, but about walking in truth and trust. I believe Cristie's book is meant for 'such a time as this.'"

LYNETTE BUNCH

"Many couples I counsel struggle with miscommunication, not because they don't love each other, but because they're often unaware of the God-given differences that shape how men and women think, feel, and respond. While agreement in every situation may not be possible, applying the lessons in this book, supported in Scripture, can lead to greater understanding, mutual validation, and deeper connection in Christ."

MARY BANAS
Marriage & Family Therapist

For Don, my strong, steady,
yet gentle, husband and partner in life.

And for everyone who wants to experience
the kind of vibrant relationships
God created them to enjoy.

INTRODUCTION

*Every part of Scripture is God-breathed and
useful one way or another—showing us truth, exposing
our rebellion, correcting our mistakes, training us to live
God's way. Through the Word we are put together and
shaped up for the tasks God has for us.*

2 Timothy 3:16-17 MSG

It was as if God began to play a movie in my mind. I could see myself
in the front flowerbed of our home. The morning summer sun beat
against the white brick house. It was hot—Texas-summer hot. I was
standing in the dry, hard dirt facing a weed that was smack dab in
the middle of the flowers.

Suddenly, this enormous weed had my full attention.

It was thick and coarse. The inside of the stem was milky white
and as sticky as glue. I tried to pull it out, but it wouldn't budge.
It was almost as tall as I am because it had been growing for a long
time. None of us had noticed it there, taking up more and more
space. But now, it reached all the way to the fascia board of the
house's trim, and it could not be ignored.

In this vision or daydream, I appeared as if I had been working
for hours. My clothes clung to my body, my hair was soaked, and

sweat stung my eyes. My hands bled from using the manual shears to wrestle with the weed. I grew increasingly frustrated and angry. How was I going to get this weed out, and why had I let it get so large?

Just then, I noticed someone nearby, casually leaning against the house, watching me. It was Jesus. His back rested on the bricks, his hands were in the pockets of his linen robe, and one ankle crossed the other. He was looking down at the dirt, but He periodically tilted His head to glance at me.

After a while, I stopped and said, "I know who You are. Why aren't You helping me?"

Jesus stood there a moment. Then He said, "You haven't asked Me. I have been watching you and waiting."

I was shocked. "Of course I want Your help! I *need* Your help. Will You please help me?"

Jesus explained that the weed had been growing in my heart because it was inherited. It had a generational root. Even though it was destructive and painful, it felt familiar. It was a weed of rebellion that would lead to deep bitterness. He emphasized that cutting down the weed would be a waste of our time; it would simply grow back. I had been going about it all wrong. Jesus gently took the manual shears from my hands.

Then He reached behind a bush and brought out a large shovel. "Are you ready to get back to work? You must do your part so I can do Mine," He said, smiling.

We began working *together*. I grabbed the weed at its base and began to rock it violently from side to side as He dug ...

Like the weed God revealed in my vision, the enemy's lies can take root in our hearts and become so big we can't cut them down to size. *Keys for Us* aims to uproot one of the lies that Satan has been planting in God's children for generations. This false belief seemed harmless enough at first, even well-meaning or admirable. But just like the weed in my vision, it has gradually taken up space, silently growing into a monstrosity that cannot be controlled and is now trying to control us.

What is that lie?

Simply put, the enemy has told us that males and females are ... the *same*.

See what I mean? At first glance, it doesn't seem so bad. Most people would find a grain of truth to agree with. We *are* the same in that males and females are both the crown of creation, God's beloved children, and heirs of the promise.

But we are fundamentally different by divine design, and ignoring our differences has gotten us into a massive mess. From an epidemic of broken marriages to a gender-confused generation, we are suffering because we don't know who we are anymore.

The culture at large doesn't articulate our differences, and the church isn't doing a good job, either.

Having been in ministry—teaching, leading, and training Bible study leaders for over thirty years—I have witnessed how this lie of "sameness" may be as deeply rooted in the Body of Christ as it is among people who don't know the Lord. Christians are supposed to be the "hospital for the hurting," but how can we help heal others when we are sick ourselves?

Males and females were created to thrive in an environment of mutual appreciation.

Instead, we're experiencing a downward spiral of mutual depreciation.

What does that look like?

Pastors sometimes joke about women from the pulpit. They think it is funny, but once our eyes are open to the plot of the enemy, things can shift.

Women sometimes roll their eyes about husbands during a Bible study. It is dishonoring to say, "I had to bring all three of my kids to the nursery with me tonight. Goodness knows my husband can't even handle one of them on his own."

Men are often painted as incompetent. Women are portrayed as overbearing. A masculine man is characterized as toxic and abusive. A feminine woman is stereotyped as overly emotional and high maintenance.

None of these depictions reflect the God in whose image we were made. No wonder we're falling apart.

In the past 30 years, we have seen a disunification in our culture, and it has bled over into the church. The enemy is using disunification to bring the opposite response that God intended for us. The specific strategies he is using are *Gender Disunification* and *Generational Disunification*. I have been shocked over the past 10 years, as these issues have surfaced all around me in ministry and culture.

Gender Disunification leads to conflict and competition instead of cooperation, respect, and partnership. It also fosters misunderstanding, mistrust, and resentment between genders. This "falsehood" has dismantled or destroyed relationships or prevented them from forming altogether. Additionally, it confuses natural differences by either erasing or weaponizing them, rather than using them as a strength.

Generational Disunification causes both older and younger people to discount or disregard one another, thereby missing out on valuable wisdom and fresh insights. This lack breaks the chain of inheritance. (Malachi 4:6) It brings oppression and destruction.

With this mindset, wisdom isn't passed down from one generation or gender to another, which breaks unity. These forms of disunity weaken families, churches, and societies. The worst result is extreme cultural chaos caused by a lack of truth, while at the very least, it results in a lack of growth and/or mental health issues.

Disunification is the weed.

The interesting thing about my vision of the flowerbed is that I don't remember ever getting rid of the weed. I think that is because Jesus loved me enough not to tell me that working on it would be a lifelong process. Generational sin is like a huge weed with deep, damaging roots. These roots don't stay the same from generation to generation. With the passage of time, the weeds get bigger, and the roots go deeper. We don't notice them until they become obvious to those around us and start to negatively affect our lives.

It doesn't have to be this way.

I have been studying masculinity and femininity for some time, and I eventually started teaching and writing about how our

God-given differences display the glorious joy God meant for us in Eden. Men and women truly make the perfect pair. It is His design.

If that is hard for you to believe right now, and if you are currently experiencing nothing but pain in your relationships with the opposite gender, there may be a generational weed growing in the soil of your heart. Identifying weeds will likely be a lifelong process for you.

However, I promise that it won't always hurt, and the reward will be worth the *work*. You will see precious connections restored, watch significant people in your life change as you change, and you will feel the power of your true identity shine forth.

Maybe you know exactly who passed down your perspective on males and females.

Maybe you aren't sure because you've not even considered it before. It's also possible that you *can't* pinpoint how you came to your current thoughts. We can be living out and activating lies we've believed without realizing it. No matter how or when the lie took root, Jesus sees it and wants to help you pull it up, and so do I. Just trust the process. It won't take as long as you think to see transformative miracles in your life.

The truth is, you were made to be a beautiful garden and leave a powerful legacy, and no weed will survive in a heart that is surrendered to the God of heaven.

Cristie Penn

Southlake, Texas

June 2025

HOW TWO PEOPLE WHO CARE ABOUT EACH OTHER CAN DRIFT APART

And this is my prayer: that your love may
abound more and more in knowledge and depth of insight,
so that you may be able to discern what is best and
may be pure and blameless for the day of Christ, filled with
the fruit of righteousness that comes through Jesus Christ
—to the glory and praise of God.

Philippians 1:9–11 NIV

Storm clouds filled the January sky. Tip-toeing across the bridal suite in my veil and white dress, I peered out the window, only to see our guests holding their hats and skirts in the blustery wind.

People clung to one another, as they tried to walk across the icy church parking lot without slipping to the pavement. This certainly wasn't the wedding weather we had wanted.

But it *was* a forecast of the turbulent days that were ahead of us.

The fact that Don and I have been married since 1979 is truly a miracle. Like most couples, we walked out of the chapel and into our future high on love, but completely unaware of the soul wounds we both carried along with our honeymoon suitcases.

We had not considered God or His plan for us; we just wanted to build a good and honest life. Yet both of us harbored unspoken and unrealistic expectations and misconceptions about marriage. And because neither of us had a personal relationship with God, we had no concept of His absolute truth, a fact that almost destroyed us.

For the first six years of marriage, we buried ourselves in our careers—I opened an interior design business while Don finished college and went to work for an engineering firm. By our seventh year of marriage, we decided to start our family. Eventually, I closed my business and focused on being a wife and mom. Don had the pressure of trying to make up my half of our income. Then, just a few years later, he opened his own engineering firm, which required long hours. We didn't realize it, but we were gradually growing apart.

In relationships, a crumbling foundation can begin with a tiny crack.

When Jonathan was two years old, a friend invited me to an Easter pageant at her church. As I watched an actor depict Jesus and the crucifixion, I realized that He had died for *me*. I went home and cried for hours, knowing I would never be the same.

Even though I'd gone to church my whole life, I did not own a Bible. For the next three years, I continued going to the church I was raised in, but I didn't have a "spiritual root system" or a deep relationship with Jesus. Therefore, when my dad, mom, and sister (my only sibling) were each diagnosed with cancer—all within three years of each other—I felt like my life was caving in.

Out of desperation, I joined Bible Study Fellowship (BSF), a weekly Bible study that meets in groups all over the world. My BSF teacher, Donna, taught me how to pray aloud and study God's Word. I began to get to know Jesus personally, and I fell in love with Him.

My dad, mom, and sister successfully completed their cancer treatments, but then my mom died suddenly from congestive heart failure. Even before my mom passed away, my parents were very upset that I attended a nondenominational Bible study like BSF. They told me I had gone off the deep end and had become a "Jesus freak." In the months before she died, my mom wouldn't even speak to me because of my faith.

She wasn't the only one. Don also began to change his attitude toward me. He became distant and withdrawn. We started fighting about petty things, and he grew increasingly frustrated with me. Most of the time, he disconnected and neglected our marriage.

We lived around the corner from my parents, and my dad repeatedly told Don I was unstable and was "doing damage" to our kids. He even accused me of being in a cult. My dad told Don he should take the kids and divorce me just to get my attention and make me snap out of it. Don trusted and respected my dad so he thought he might be right. Don had not yielded his life to Christ at the time, and the enemy used my own family to gain a foothold and try to destroy our marriage. I felt violated, betrayed, ambushed, and completely alone, which only caused me to press deeper into Jesus.

All I could do was pray and trust God with my future.

For years, there was a constant spiritual battle in our home. Part of the problem was that I had developed some false beliefs. I thought Christian women were to figuratively "wash the feet" of their husbands, faithfully wait on their every need, and pray for their salvation ... in *silence*. I hoped that if I lived in quiet servitude and never expressed a complaint, Don would come to Christ. I thought it was my responsibility to be an example of Jesus to my entire family, which made me desperately try to be "the perfect Christian woman." This may have sounded good on the surface, but when I did not see any change in Don, I became angry and bitter at him, God, and myself.

Over time, Don's emotional absence brought fear, which caused me to self-protect and isolate. I crawled deeper and deeper into an emotional hole. As I pulled away and grew into a passive, hurt female, our partnership broke and our relationship suffered. I stopped being the fun, exciting girl he fell in love with. This "new me" did not make my husband want to become a follower of Christ. To him, I'd become a robot, a shadow of the woman he once knew.

I didn't mean for it to happen. I thought I was doing the right thing. I did not understand that Don's salvation would take a supernatural work of the Holy Spirit and had nothing to do with me. I also didn't realize I was unconsciously trying to manipulate Don ... and God.

But Don had an encounter with Jesus in spite of me. When a friend invited him to the BSF men's Bible study, he got to know Jesus personally. And just like me, he fell in love with Him.

By then, Don had built a thriving engineering company, and together we stayed busy raising our kids. Things had changed for the better when we both became Christians, but we had not yet unpacked our personal baggage or found freedom from years of our extended families' drama.

I justified my continued self-protection toward my husband and kept thinking to myself, *Don and I are better than ever, right? We are leading a small group and studying the Bible together. Doesn't that mean things are great?*

But our marriage didn't feel that great. I knew Don and I were not as close as we could be. God's redeeming work in our marriage had only just begun.

The Lord revealed the root issue to me when our daughter Holly fell in love with a handsome young man named Jon. It was a delight to watch our college-aged daughter discover a love that could last a lifetime. But during their courtship I began to sense sadness settling in my heart.

From time to time, I would pray and ask the Lord, "What is this I am feeling?" He was silent on the subject until after Jon and Holly's wedding day.

The happy couple headed toward their honeymoon, and I sat down with a deep sigh that only a mother-of-the-bride can make. The ballroom was empty, the candles were dark, and the flowers were gone. I was overjoyed for Holly and Jon, but my sadness was still there.

A few weeks later, God finally pulled back the curtain.

"Cristie, this sadness you have been feeling for months is grief," He said. "This has nothing to do with Holly and her prince charming and everything to do with the way you view yours."

At that moment, my mind's eye could see the way that Jon looked at Holly, and the way Holly responded to Jon. He was her champion and her hero, and he knew it. It had been decades since Don and I had looked at each other with such adoration. Where had my prince gone? Had I done anything to make him step away from his position as hero of the household? It broke my heart to think about how things had changed between us.

If I were honest, I did see Don as a knight and a warrior. However, instead of standing by my side to fight for me, he stood across the arena with his shield and sword drawn against me.

We were once so in love. How had we become opponents?

Over the coming days, I scooted closer to the Lord in my spirit and began to search His Word, be still, and listen carefully. I diligently looked for the truth and asked Him for the courage to see what He wanted me to see. It was as though the Father had lovingly pulled me up into His lap and held me close.

The Lord asked me a lot of hard questions during my moments alone with Him: "Do you believe Don is a kind man with good intentions? Do you believe he wants the best for you and your family? Is he still the most valuable gift I have ever given to you? Will you stop trying to protect yourself? Will you be vulnerable with him? Will you trust him? Will you trust *Me*?"

I knew I had a choice to make. I could not change my husband, but with God's help, I could change the way I viewed him.

Fear ripped through me. What if Don hurt me again, shut down, or verbally and emotionally ignored me or attacked me? What if I put my heart on the line and nothing changed? The kids were out of the house and on their own, which took away all my emotional buffers and distractions. I had nowhere to hide. It was just the two of us, and I was so afraid.

But I was willing and teachable.

Then something interesting happened. The more I opened myself to the work God was doing in my heart, the less it was about me. I began to envision the countless women I had known over the course of my life. As their faces passed through my mind, I noticed something familiar. They made it look like everything was great on the outside, but on the inside, they were lonely, hurt, angry, and, in some cases, bitter. They too had been hoping for meaningful connection with their husbands, brothers, and male colleagues. Sadly, the opposite had become true. Men and women were at war with each other. The aching need was deep, and I was eager to learn why, even if the discovery process had to start with me.

"Okay, Lord. I'll follow You," I prayed. "Show me what to do."

Almost immediately, the Lord began revealing the "next right thing" to do as I related to Don. The restoration of my heart had begun. I simply tried to obey exactly as God directed, taking steps forward one day—one moment—at a time.

I did my best to unselfishly follow His direction without expectations for six months. Then one day, Don told me that he wasn't sure what I was up to, but he liked it. Our marriage had started to improve because God was slowly repositioning our hearts toward each other. Even though we still had a learning curve and a lot of work to do.

Then God showed me a metaphor of Don and me.

In the vision, I was a little girl, pulling a red wagon up a well-traveled, muddy hill. The harder I worked, the more I sweated and strained. I knew God was at the top of the mountain. When I took a closer look, I could see the wagon was sinking in the mud because the load was too heavy. To my surprise, the heavy load was Don!

He was a little boy who had on royal blue shorts and cowboy boots. He was sitting in the back of the wagon, looking down the mountain and dragging his boots in the mud. The more his boots became caked with mud, the harder it was for me to pull.

Then, I heard the Lord speak from the top of the mountain, "Cristie, drop the handle of the wagon. Let it go."

I was so afraid to let it go. If I dropped the handle, what would happen to Don? We hadn't reached the top of the mountain yet. He might never know God the way I wanted him to.

The Lord spoke again, "If you don't drop the handle you're not trusting Me, and you are in My way. Sometimes when Don is cruel to you, it's because he's angry with Me. You are standing between us, and I can't get to him. With you in the way, he can't see Me."

That was the day I chose to "drop the handle of the wagon," and our marriage has never been the same. God took our struggling relationship and transformed us into the loving partners and companions He created us to be.

And if He did it for us, He can do it for you, too.

WHAT'S HAPPENED TO OUR HEARTS?

Be very careful, then, how you live—not as unwise
but as wise, making the most of every opportunity because
the days are evil. Therefore do not be foolish, but
understand what the Lord's will is.

Ephesians 5:15-17 NIV

Deep inside, women know they need men, and men know they need women, but it has become socially unacceptable to admit it aloud. If we were to go out on the street or eavesdrop on conversations in restaurants or coffee shops, how often would we hear women praising men, or men praising women? When was the last time you overheard a group of females honoring the masculinity of the men in their lives and appreciating their strength? When was the last time you listened to a group of men honoring the confident femininity of their wives or female colleagues?

Instead, we are inundated with terms like "toxic masculinity" and phrases like "The future is female." Most of the time when one gender is talking about the other, the comments are critical. Men tend to think women are high maintenance and emotionally indulgent, and women often assume men are out of touch with their feelings.

What do you imagine God thinks about this trend?

The Bible says, "the Creator originally made man and woman *for* each other" (Matthew 19:4, MSG, emphasis mine). I'm sure it makes Him very sad to see His kids with a completely different mindset. We cannot be *for* each other when we are against each other. He knows this perspective leaves us unprotected and lonely, looking for a true partner to join us in the valleys and victories of life.

We were made to *complete* each other, not *compete* with each other.

Whether you are married or single, the conflict is real. It's in our homes, offices, and yes, in some cases, even in churches and organizations that bear the name of Jesus. It's even on our televisions, with the scripts of commercials or sitcoms displaying the husband as goofy or the clown and females as the wise, eye-rolling, teacher-type who tolerates them.

Are either one of those roles who you really want to be? In *Bringing Up Girls,* Dr. James Dobson writes,

Between 1965 and 1995, some of the most highly educated and sophisticated people drew the conclusion that males and females were different only with regard to reproductive anatomy and physiology. The prevailing view was that every other distinguishing feature between the sexes had resulted from patriarchal upbringing. Boys, it was said, were coerced into being traditionally masculine, which was a serious problem for society. That belief, promoted with great passion by what was then called the Women's Liberation Movement, served to blind most psychiatrists, psychologists, neurologists, pediatricians, educators, politicians, writers, social activists, television personalities such as Phil Donahue and Barbara Walters, and millions of mothers and fathers throughout the Western world ... How could boys and girls be identical if their DNA is different?... The prevailing belief had been dead wrong.

When Jesus rescued me from myself, I began asking Him how the church had veered so far from His beautiful design in the beginning. With each generation, our collective history keeps moving us further and further away from *His vision for us*. When society had a diminished view of females prior to and during the 1950s, many women stuffed their emotional pain. This may have led to anger, rebellion, protests, and the sexual revolution of the 1960s. The pendulum of correction swung too far in the opposite direction. That pendulum was set in motion from the broken hearts of women who had felt unheard, disrespected, and underpaid for far too long. Their anguish was real, but their cries for help have become seen as militant and demanding. Women started burning bras, refusing to take their husband's names, and singing songs with lyrics like "I can bring home the bacon [and] fry it up in the pan" or "I am woman, hear me roar."

Men, who were created by God to be hunters, warriors, and kings looked upon a new generation of women who were acting like men. As a result, the men lost their confidence, gave up, and dropped their swords. Women were communicating that they didn't need men anymore. So males stopped fighting for the females in their lives because the message was clear: females could fight for themselves. Without the presence of godly masculinity in the community, women started to feel even worse. They now often feel invisible, ignored, abandoned, and exposed. Over time, women became even louder and more aggressive out of pain and fear. Deep inside, there was a war going on. TRUTH: They ceased to feel safe.

In other words, women have picked up the swords that men have dropped, choosing to protect themselves and their children with a weapon that was never fitted to them. They believed the lie that they have to force their way into being valued, cherished, and respected. But when women try to force it, men pull away. And the painful cycle can continue for generations.

In her book, *Men and Women in the Church*, author Sarah Sumner explains,

Secular feminists are keenly aware of the physical disparity that exists between women and men, but some don't like to talk about it for fear that any recognition of the difference between men's and women's strength will be used politically as an argument for male superiority. Thus they'd rather emphasize the common humanity of men and women. Evangelical feminists tend to have a similar point of view. As one Christian woman put it, 'Men just so happen to be gendered as males, and women just so happen to be gendered as females. But basically, we're all just people.' Another biblical feminist told me it's "un-strategic" to talk about the differences between men and women. She said that saying the word different ushers in a "death sentence" to the global cause of women's concerns ... I can understand this woman's determination to be cautious. It is un-strategic politically for women to say that women are different from men. The problem is that when women are seen as different, men are seen as normal. The rationale flows like this: Men are normal. Women are not men. Women are not normal.

Damaging beliefs will affect coming generations if we don't have the courage to learn how to take up our God-designed identities and speak truth in love. The line of distinction between men and women has become increasingly blurred. Many are confused about manhood and womanhood, and many parents don't know how to develop gender-specific strengths in their children. Freedom comes when we accept that men and women are different by design and created to complement one another. Whether married or single, women need men, men need women, and there's no reason to be ashamed.

Recently I spoke about this concept at a church, and after the class, a small group of middle-aged singles, both males and females, approached me to talk about what they had just heard.

A man said, "Thank you so much for giving single men permission to be brothers to the single women in our group of friends. We see they need help, but they rarely let us help them, and we are afraid we will offend them if we ask."

A woman next to him added, "We are afraid to look weak. We need to trust men more and let them know when we need their masculinity. I don't understand why we aren't comfortable with that."

Many women think it is a sign of weakness to let a man help them. Some even assume if they let men help, the men will expect something in return. It's important for women to remember that good-hearted men just want to operate in their unique abilities and strengths because they are wired to do so. Men aren't always expecting repayment when they offer to help. It's time to change those stereotypes. Yes, change can be hard, even when we are aching and begging for it. But it is possible.

Remember what it took for my marriage to be transformed?

All the Lord needed was my willingness to "drop the handle of the wagon," and He took it from there. No matter whom you have been pulling up a hill, God's generous offer stands for you, as well. Give Him your willingness and follow Him one day—even one moment—at a time. He will reveal your "next right thing" to do.

To help you know where to begin, I will share three foundational concepts that I started practicing in my relationships with
men—first with my husband and then with other males in my life.
The positive effects of these three concepts are undeniable. Eventually, I began to wonder: *If these truths work so well for men, are
there other truths that can benefit women?*

I thank the Lord that there are.

These revelations are simple, but they have profoundly impacted
our marriage, our friends, and our adult children so much that Don
encouraged—yes, even kindly pushed—me to write them down to
share with others.

I call these foundational concepts the keys. Before I reveal them
later in the book, it's important to remind you that they are effective when embraced by imperfect people who have reasonable
emotional health. Unhealthy people should not use these keys to
become abusive and manipulative because they have a warped sense
of God's design. And no one should use these keys as a reason to
stay in an abusive situation. Please, if you're not sure, seek godly,
professional counsel and help.

One more thing, as you read through the keys, you may not
immediately relate to or want to accept them. That is when your
willingness to trust God comes into play. Listen and obey. He will
never steer you in the wrong direction. This path may feel unfamil-
iar at first, but it will lead you to freedom. My prayer is that you
will experience the beautifully restored relationships that God has
waiting for you on the other side.

DIFFERENT BY DESIGN

Submit to one another out of reverence for Christ.

Ephesians 5:21 NIV

When Don and I built a new home, I witnessed masculinity on display. Early in the project, I became fascinated when I would walk the property every day, meeting with the builder. There was a constant flurry of activity. Whether the men were on the lot moving dirt, hoisting lumber, setting huge slabs of granite, pulling electrical wires in the hot attic, or hanging chandeliers and cabinets, they captivated me with their strength. Nothing was too heavy for some brawn or machinery to manipulate into position. Whatever I desired was the project manager's command, and I marveled to see them execute difficult tasks with ease. The men didn't seem to mind walking around in muddy work boots or tossing lumber, bricks, and shingles to one another while standing on high, shaky scaffolding. They didn't look bothered by the scorching August sun or the freezing December rain. And eating outside with dirt-caked hands or using a portable toilet? They were unfazed.

They had no idea how much I was admiring and appreciating them every day. During the building process, the men were on a mission to get the job done, and they did it with grit, sweat, muscle, and masculine determination—especially if they knew a female might be watching.

This experience was memorable because by then the position of my heart was so different. I was seeing men through a new lens. Our home-building project became a real-life research lab for me. As I observed the men work, it further solidified my already strong belief that women need men. Imagine trying to build a home without them? Sure, it's possible, but it would take a whole lot more time, and possibly more machinery. That is not a criticism of women, it is a measurable fact.

Men and women bring different skills and interests for the benefit of all. It has nothing to do with societal pressure or cultural expectations. For instance, when our children were young, Don and I gave them the freedom to play in any way they desired. If our son, Jonathan, found an empty box when he was a child, he would kick it or stand on it. He was trying to test its durability to see what kind of pressure it took to crush it. Sometimes, he'd use it as a stool to stand on as he guarded his kingdom in an imaginary battle. On the other hand, if our daughter, Holly, found an empty box, she would carry it around the house looking for items to put inside. She would thoughtfully arrange the objects in the box and place the lid securely on top.

Whatever ended up inside that box was her treasure.

My son and daughter were different from day one. When we take a moment to observe children, it's easy to see God's design. We should recognize that at every age there are some obvious and somewhat extreme physical differences between males and females. These differences were built into each gender for a purpose.

A woman may be taller than a man, but even so, she might not be able to overpower him because of his natural muscle mass and bone density. Women don't have the same testosterone levels as men, which makes male muscles and bones different from female muscles and bones. No matter how hard women may try, they just don't have the same structure—down to the cell—to do what men are designed to do.

The first step to understanding God's design for the sexes is to see how He created us from the beginning. So, let's look at what the Creator of the Universe may have had in mind when He designed men and women in the Garden of Eden.

As soon as the earth was stable enough to sustain life, "God said, 'Let Us make man in Our image, according to Our likeness; let them have dominion over ... every living thing that moves on the earth'" (Genesis 1:26–28, NKJV).

Notice that God did not say, "Let males have dominion over females," yet this is what many people assume He meant. Healthy, godly men do not want to dominate women; they want to partner with them.

How do we know that a woman is the perfect partner for a man? The Bible explains,

> "The Lord God formed the man from the dust of the ground. He breathed the breath of life into the man's nostrils, and the man became a living person. The Lord God said, 'It is not good for the man to be alone. I will make a helper who is *just right* for him.' So the Lord God formed from the ground all the wild animals and all the birds of the sky. He brought them to the man to see what he would call them, and the man chose a name for each one ... but still there was no helper *just right* for him. So the Lord God caused the man to fall into a deep sleep. While the man slept, the Lord God took out one of the man's ribs and closed up the opening. Then the Lord God made a woman from the rib, and he brought her to the man. 'At last!' the man exclaimed. 'This one is bone from my bone, and flesh from my flesh! She will be called "woman," because she was taken from "man"'" (Genesis 2:7, 18–23 NLT, emphasis mine).

Even though Adam was in the presence of God, he still *needed* a "just right" companion. Think about it, when we are in God's perfect presence, we don't need anything, unless God creates the need within us. Christians often say, "God is enough. I don't need a wife. Or I don't need a husband." Others might feel selfish because they want a wife or a husband so badly. But the male-female partnership is not just a *want*. God knew that Adam *needed* someone else, a helpmate.

The companion God made for Adam was not made from his head, to rule over him.

Neither was she made from his feet, to be walked on by him. Adam's helper was made from his side, to live safely beside him and under his arm of protection and provision. God wanted to deliver Eve to Adam as a gift, not as a possession. She was meant to be a queen, not a slave.

Do you think God had planned to give Eve to Adam all along? While the Bible doesn't say Adam verbally asked for Eve, maybe the Lord wanted to let Adam feel the desire so he would be ready to receive her as a precious treasure. The Lord may have wanted this recorded so that men and women would realize, even from the beginning, He loves to give us the desires of our hearts (Psalm 20:4; Psalm 37:4).

We see a beautiful representation of this Edenic moment in Christian weddings today. The bride is escorted down the aisle by her father (or by someone important to her) to stand in for her heavenly Father. The expectant bridegroom waits to receive her as his treasure. I believe our Heavenly Father delights in giving a bride to a bridegroom because it is a picture of what He longs to do for Jesus when He is united with His Bride (see Revelation 19:7-9).

When a bridegroom has not taken the bride sexually before she has been given to him, God is delighted, and His presence fills the atmosphere. Sadly, our culture suggests that men should do the opposite. If a man wants a woman, he can sleep with her, even if she is not his. Instead of men covering and protecting women from making mistakes that can lead to unwanted pregnancies, single parenting, diseases, abortions, brokenness, rejection, loneliness, and many other things, they are making women vulnerable to those things.

The message for women in today's culture isn't any better. Too many women discount their value and worth by giving themselves away before they're married. The problem with that is we don't belong to ourselves; we belong to God. He is the only one who can give away a bride in marriage. When men and women experience physical intimacy with one another before it is time, it breaks God's heart because it goes against His original plan for us. The Giver wants to be the One to initiate the giving. First Corinthians 6:19–20 (NLT) says, "Don't you realize that your body is the temple of the Holy Spirit, who lives in you and was given to you by God? You do not belong to yourself, for God bought you with a high price. So you must honor God with your body."

I'll never forget one wedding where we saw this truth in living color. When the back doors of the chapel opened, the bride and her father entered the doorway and began to make their way down the aisle. Every eye was on her, and she seemed uncomfortable with the attention.

Then she locked eyes with her groom. It was a beautiful thing to witness, as the faint smile on her face became a look of complete contentment. Almost without blinking, she continued down the aisle, holding tightly to her daddy's arm.

As she moved closer to the front of the church, her groom broke down. Bending at the waist, with one hand over his face, he began to weep. He was so grateful for the beautiful gift approaching him that he could not contain his emotion.

When a couple honors God by not taking one another sexually until they've made a covenant with Him, I believe God is eager to come and be the Master of the Ceremony. He wants us to have the best He has to offer: a spouse as a holy gift from Him.

If you have gotten this out of order, know that you can trust God and repent, believing He is gracious. There is no condemnation for those who are in Christ Jesus. We all can get a fresh start and a new slate when we yield and ask Him to restore us. But we must be willing to come back to His plan whenever we step outside of it. Yes, God's plan and purpose for Adam and Eve is still in place today. He will not change His mind. Men will always need women, and women will always need men.

At this point, you may be thinking, "I'm different. I don't fit into the male or female definitions described so far."

I get it. In the beginning of this process, I thought, *I am more like a man in some ways. I'm independent and strong*. Does this describe you, too? In some ways, you may feel you've switched roles. Based on my experience, more than a few men behave more like women, and some women behave more like men. The reasons for this could be their upbringing, the environment they grew up in, or the people they are in relationships with. There are boys who are artistic and creative, but they do these things in a masculine way because their masculinity has been called forth and developed. There are girls who are athletes or tomboys, but their femininity is fully developed and intact. Genetics and environments make a difference in how boys and girls see and express themselves.

Growing up, I was a tomboy and was proud of it! One of my favorite things to do was go out on the boat with my dad. He was an airline pilot and often had weekdays off, which gave us the opportunity to go out to the lake on days it wasn't as crowded.

On one particular day, there weren't any other boats out on the lake, and the water was as smooth as glass. When we got the boat out to the center of the lake, my dad threw his ski into the water, followed by a rope, and then he jumped in.

"You're going to pull me," he shouted up to me.

I had driven the boat often, but to drive it solo with no one else in the boat was horrifying to me. I was only 11 years old.

Doubting my abilities, questions flooded my mind: *What if I run over him when it's time to circle around and pick him up? What if he falls? What if he gets hurt?*

My dad kept saying, "Would I ask you to do anything I don't know you can do?" He had more faith in me than I had in myself.

From that point forward, I drove the boat and trailered it with ease. I even learned how to pull off boat motors and rebuild them on the boat dock with my dad's help. And it wasn't long before I knew every tool in his garage. My dad felt it was important for me, as a female, to be independent and strong. And I did, too.

God is much too creative to make each of us exactly alike. The focus of the following section is not on each gender's character traits; it's on God's original purpose and position for males and females. Stereotypes and pre-judgments can confuse you or trip you up. Just stay open and listen to what the Holy Spirit is saying to you about you. Keep asking the Lord if you have adapted to something you were not built for.

First, let's look at the distinctions, or differences, between males and females.

MALE FUNCTION:	FEMALE FUNCTION:
• Hunter (Provider) • Warrior (Protector) • King (Leader)	• Collector (Beautifier) • Connector (Nurturer) • Queen (Co-Leader)

MALE ORIGIN:	FEMALE ORIGIN:
• Dirt (Refined Rock)	• Flesh and Bone

MALE COMPOSITION:	FEMALE COMPOSITION:
• Solid (Like Rock)	• Fluid (Like Water)

MALE EMOTIONAL OPERATION:	FEMALE EMOTIONAL OPERATION:
• Single-Focused (Telescope)	• Multi-Tasked (Radar)

MALE PRIMARY NEED:	FEMALE PRIMARY NEED:
• Honor and Respect	• Protection and Provision

MALE AND FEMALE FUNCTIONS EXPLAINED

God Designed Men To Be Hunters, Warriors, and Kings

From the moment boys can walk they're becoming hunters, warriors, and kings. Boys are relentlessly looking for ways to demonstrate their power, strength, and ability. They look for opportunities to battle, conquer, climb, and compete. Ladies, when you look at the men in your life, consider this: There is always a little boy full of adventure inside of them. Wives, inside the man you married is a little boy who would still climb the highest mountain and scrape up his knees and elbows, striving until his hands were bruised and bloodied just to get to the top and prove to you he is worthy of your respect and affection. He's designed to show you his masculinity, and he'll never outgrow it. He is wired to be a king. This God-given trait is there to make you feel secure.

God Designed Women To Be Collectors, Connectors, and Queens

Baby girls come out of the womb looking for ways to collect and connect with people, places, and things. A little girl's desire to be cherished and cared for is bonded to the healthy affection of her daddy. She longs to see the delight in his eyes as she gracefully curtseys in front of him. Men, when you look at a woman, consider this: There is always a little girl who desires to be told she's beautiful and valued. That same little girl who played dress up with her mommy's clothes is the one who now gets dressed up for you and hopes you will notice how pretty she is. She values your opinion because she has a desire to please you. She's designed to connect with you, and she'll never outgrow it. This God-given trait is there to make you feel secure, too.

MALE AND FEMALE COMPOSITIONS EXPLAINED

God Designed The Male Composition As "Solid"

I find it very interesting that God could create the first human being out of anything, but He chose to make Adam from dirt. Why not make the first man from light? Or water? Because without dirt, a seed will not have a safe, protected environment to take root and grow.

Dirt is refined rock. You may have even heard someone say, "That man is solid as a rock." Science recognizes and acknowledges that the male is the physically stronger of the two genders. Men's testosterone levels bring abundant strength and other physical differences. They have a built-in desire for adventure, exploration, and competition.

Most men enjoy being outside hunting, boating, golfing, camping, playing sports, or competing in some way.

God Designed The Female Composition As "Fluid"

The first female was not made from dirt but fashioned from Adam's rib. She was composed of a man's bone and flesh. Let's look at what that symbolizes. Bone is the rigid tissue that makes up the skeleton, while flesh is the soft connective tissue of the body that holds it together. Is it any wonder that the Lord would use both rigid and soft connective tissue to make the first female? It is the strength of the skeleton and the agility of the connective tissue that makes a human body fluid.

Women naturally bring together and hold people, places, and things spiritually and emotionally. Like bone, when a woman is healthy emotionally and physically, she can bend instead of break. But when women are not nurtured, nourished, provided for, and protected, they can become brittle and sometimes shatter.

MALE AND FEMALE EMOTIONAL OPERATIONS EXPLAINED

God Created The Male Emotional Operation To Work Like A Telescope

Most males are single-focused, meaning they can usually only focus on one thing at a time. They have the intensity of a telescope. It's not easy for men to be doing one thing and immediately switch and be completely engaged in something else. If a man is cleaning the garage, his focus is on cleaning the garage. If he is watching sports, he is watching sports. This explains why some men resist having an intimate conversation while they are driving because his focus is on the road and arriving to his destination safely and on time. (Remember, he is wired as a warrior and a hunter. He gets the job done.) Men are designed by God to fully engage in one thing at a time. His telescopic focus is of great value to him and to others in his life, both at home and at work.

God Created The Female Emotional Operation To Work Like A Radar

Women are multi-taskers. It seems as though women have a built-in radar that allows them to sense danger, assess new opportunities, collect, connect to beauty, multiply, and see the needs of the people around them—all at the same time. A woman is constantly aware of what is going on around her. A female's radar is not usually turned off unless she is asleep. (Even then, she's usually the first to hear a child cry.) Her multi-tasking radar is of great value to her and to others in her life, both at home and at work.

MALE AND FEMALE PRIMARY NEEDS EXPLAINED

God Created Males To Need Honor And Respect

Men desire to be recognized and appreciated for their value and worth, so when allowed to protect and provide, they feel honor and respect. Many times men feel dishonored and disrespected because the women in their lives do not allow them to protect and provide for them, which emasculates them and strips them of their purpose.

Thankfully, salaries for women have increased over the years, giving them the chance to earn as much or more than men. However, as these opportunities have grown, a dismissive attitude toward men may have grown along with them. Many women are in self-preservation mode and take pride in saying things like, "I can do this myself" or "I don't need a man to provide for me." This type of perspective creates confusion, and males react by disengaging or shutting down altogether. No matter how strong men may seem or how confident they are, deep down inside their primary need is honor and respect. They want to know they are valued by women, and they are wired to be dependable. It hurts them at their core when a woman they love or admire refuses to depend on or acknowledge their strength, which is there for her benefit.

God Created Females To Need Protection And Provision

Women are designed to feel secure, nurtured, and cherished by the men in their lives (fathers, husbands, friends, etc.). This kind of security is what makes a woman thrive. Women want respect too, but the reasons are different. Her need for respect is often related to her need to be cherished and safe. The bottom line is that God created women to receive what men need to give.

In the following chapters, we will explore these differences in detail. For now, ask yourself an important question. If there were a way to experience joy, peace, and meaningful communication in your relationships with the opposite gender, would you want it? You can have what you long for, but—I'll say it again—it requires your willingness to trust God and believe that He created us to need what only the other gender can provide.

It's okay if you don't *feel* willing, yet. Willingness is a decision that you can make before you feel like it. Trust me, your feelings will follow, and by the time they do, you'll be experiencing blessings that you can only imagine right now.

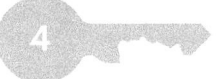

DIFFERENT FOR A PURPOSE

*But we ought always to thank God for you, brothers
and sisters loved by the Lord, because God chose you as
firstfruits to be saved through the sanctifying work of the
Spirit and through belief in the truth.*

2 Thessalonians 2:13 NIV

Picture a potter at the potter's wheel. He's ready to create a one-of-a-kind mug. He begins by placing a large, damp lump of clay onto the wheel. As the lump of cold, wet clay turns faster and faster, the potter forms the shape by applying pressure from the outside. After a few seconds, the potter also begins to apply pressure to the inside by forcing his hand down into the lump of clay. Constantly dipping his hands in water to keep the clay wet, the potter applies balanced pressure from the inside out, which creates a void, or a hole, in the vessel.

Now, the clay has purpose.

When it is dry, it is dipped and fired in an intensely hot kiln, which makes it strong and resilient. A substance that used to be indistinguishable has become indispensable. It is a hollow vessel, ready for service. A mug is solid, durable, and rugged. Glazed and fired for strength, a clay mug is not translucent and can withstand heat, pressure, and sudden jolts. It may chip, but it rarely shatters.

Like clay mugs, men can only hold (focus on) one thing at a time. They are strong, insulated, durable, and unembellished. Masculine men are designed to be physically and functionally solid, rugged, and formed from dirt. Who made them that way?

Isaiah 64:8 says, "Yet you, Lord, are our Father. We are the clay, you are the potter; we are all the work of your hand" (NIV).

God formed men with the same intentionality that a potter forms a mug. And just like a mug must be filled with something in order to attain its intended purpose, a man must be filled by the Holy Spirit in order to fulfill his purpose and full potential.

You could probably continue thinking of revelations about men and their attentive Potter all day, but it's just as fascinating to shift the metaphor and look at the making of a crystal pitcher.

What makes a crystal pitcher different from a glass pitcher is the lead that's added to the glass to make it more clear, pure, radiant, and less of a blue/green color. The lead crystal is subjected to intense heat in a furnace and at the perfect time, the molten—or heat-softened glass—is held at the end of a blowpipe (a hollow, stainless steel tube), and a master glassblower shapes it with his breath. Then he uses a steel tool called a marver to cool and shape the molten glass. Finally, the glassblower places a handle on the side of the pitcher and uses water and a circular saw to cut ridges into the crystal.

Cutting ridges adds character to the design and produces a colorful prismatic effect.

When the light passes through the pitcher at different angles, the light refracts and separates into a visible spectrum, creating a stunning rainbow.

Like a crystal pitcher, the heart of a woman is formed by the breath of God. They are fragile and delicate by nature. The smallest jolt can cause their trust to shatter. They are clear and transparent; you can easily see what's inside. And just like the deep cuts and ridges on a crystal pitcher refract light, women must allow the Light of Jesus to fill their hearts in order to bring out their true, sparkling beauty, purpose, and full potential.

Think about it for a moment. A mug is not more or less important than a crystal pitcher, and vice versa. The two vessels were simply created for very similar but very different purposes. Yes, they both are made for liquid. However, a crystal pitcher could not hold scalding hot coffee or withstand the turbulence of a dishwasher, and a mug handles these things every day. A clay mug could not be a part of a beautiful tablescape or create a special, celebratory atmosphere, and a crystal pitcher can do the job with ease.

The same is true about men and women. We were made for very similar but very different purposes. Let's look at how God uses the opposite gender as tools in His hands to sanctify us.

Sanctification is a big word for the process God uses to make us holy and transform us into the likeness of Christ. Sanctification only happens when Christians are in relationship with each other and with Christ. The Holy Spirit most often uses the marriage relationship to accomplish this. Yet, amazingly, we don't have to be married in order for the Lord to use the opposite gender to sanctify us; our differences are built in to help us and teach us through friends, colleagues, and relatives, as well.

As we discussed in the previous chapter, men are born to be providers, protectors, and leaders. By nature, they are not nurturing or tender, but through the sanctification process, they can become more like Christ, developing into a king who wields a sword of protection in one hand while nurturing like a tender shepherd with the other. The more men have the character and attributes of Christ, the more natural nurturing and tenderness become to them.

How can a woman be sanctified by interacting with a man who is submitted to God's design for him? Well, in today's world, it doesn't feel safe for her to drop the sword and stop providing for and protecting herself. For a woman, the sanctification process is learning to trust, to yield to Christ, and to believe that God will position men in her life who will provide for and protect her. She must learn to trust the men God has placed in her life and lay down the sword of self-protection and self-defense.

God's design for women is to be beautifiers, nurturers, and co-leaders. A woman collects information and connects with people, places, and things all day, every day. She goes to work, enjoys friends, runs errands, and manages a household and the schedules of everyone who lives in it. This elegant role has historically been referred to as "the Lady of the House." In other words, she is a queen with the privilege of being everywhere at the same time—her radar is always on, and her list is endless. Because of this, at the end of her day, it's important she has the opportunity to "pour out" what she's collected in her soul. Her soul is her crystal pitcher.

How can a man be sanctified by interacting with a woman submitted to God's design for her? He can patiently invite her to pour out her soul by listening and showing attention and care. This practice helps him become more like Jesus—our nurturing and tender Shepherd.

Men, God doesn't want you to lay down your swords or cease to be hunters and warriors.

That is who you were created to be. He doesn't plan to strip you of your masculinity. He plans for you to be a sanctified warrior with the heart of a nurturing and tender shepherd. It's not what you do but how you do it.

Women, God doesn't want you to cease being beautifiers and nurturers. It is who you were created to be. He wants you to stop being your own provider and protector; that is emasculating to real men. He hopes you will make room for a man, a tender shepherd, who will step in and cover you. This could be a husband, friend, brother, or any other man who is willing to fill this role.

When we learn the needs of both genders and begin to understand their wiring, we can't help but see that we were designed to balance one another. In fact, when we are aligned, we fit together like a zipper. I like to call this the "zipper effect."

Everyone knows what a zipper looks like, but it's worth noting that a zipper has a slider that either interlocks or separates the toothed tracks. Like a zipper, we are meant to interlock with each other to bring supernatural unity and support. But when we are not partnering with the Lord and each other, we're being pulled and separated. Satan is the author of confusion, and his plan is to diminish our differences and convince us to be more alike so we don't need one another or, even worse, become adversaries.

God's original plan cannot be altered by what society thinks or suggests. Culture does not determine the truth. When we accept our identities and interlock with the Lord and each other, we become unified. We fit together, like a zipper, locking out the enemy and his lies.

After Satan targeted the weakness and selfishness of Adam and Eve and provided them with the opportunity to sin, God "said to the serpent: 'Because you have done this, you are cursed more than all cattle, and more than every beast of the field; on your belly you shall go, and you shall eat dust all the days of your life'" (Genesis 3:14, NKJV). Did you catch it? Satan was cursed to eat dust all the days of his life. Why is that significant? Because Adam, the first human created, was made from dust. If Satan is restricted to eating only dust (what Adam's flesh was made from), could it be that we are feeding the enemy and making him stronger when we act on our fleshly desires by choosing to sin?

The king of counterfeit is trying to shift the enmity (hostility, hate, antagonism, animosity, ill will) that God placed between Satan and us, to enmity between us and God. And also between men and women. As long as we have breath, we have the awesome privilege of working for and with one another to reflect the Father to every heart on the planet. God wired our hearts with a need to know Him as Savior, but we also need one another to be a complete representation of the Father. We were designed to work beautifully together to reflect the royal personhood of the Trinity.

Men and women are different but both reflect equally powerful and important parts of God and His character. Women are the feminine, nurturing, gentle side of God and fit safely under the provision and protection of the masculine, warrior side of God.

We must recognize Satan is not omnipresent and can't read our minds or our futures, but he and his demons study our behavior. I wonder if Satan noticed that Eve was designed by his enemy, God, to gravitate toward beauty. Women of all ages are wired to do this. They collect pieces (sometimes the broken pieces of their lives or someone else's life) and try to create something beautiful from them. Much like a mosaic artist tries to make a beautiful picture, plate, or piece of furniture out of broken pieces of china or glass, a woman sees the potential in people and tries to cultivate it into something lovely. Women are compelled to do this; however, she sometimes needs the balance of men to help keep her out of a ditch. The very things God put inside her as a gift, if not sifted constantly through the guidance and direction of the Holy Spirit and some form of accountability, can destroy her and those she cares about, as it did with Eve.

Sometimes women do not comprehend the mysterious complexities of their nature or the powerful influence they have over the males in their lives. This is why a woman needs the strength of a man to balance her. There are times when women don't fully understand what's going on in their bodies. Hormonal changes beyond her control cause her to have emotions that are sometimes embarrassing and, in some cases, scary. For instance, her monthly cycle, pregnancy, and menopause make her feel out of control. Her body is constantly evolving. A woman's physiology causes emotional and physical changes that can be challenging to manage and difficult for her to anticipate. There are times when she may not have a warning that changes are coming or how to deal with them. The fluctuation of her emotions is often caused by hormonal changes she doesn't understand.

As hunters and warriors, men usually automatically conceal instead of choosing to reveal.

They tend to have a hard time letting down their guard and being vulnerable with the women who care about them. When a man learns how to reveal his feelings, the women in his life experience the emotional intimacy, security, and nurturing they need.

Tears are nothing to be ashamed of when sharing authentic feelings. A man's humility and authenticity will open a female heart to him. This results in her trusting him and creates a strong sense of partnership.

The Lord knew it would be a challenge for men to be verbally vulnerable, but He may have planned to use this challenge as a transformation tool, making them more like Jesus. Men love a challenge, and most seek to conquer it.

I believe with all my heart most men really want to get this right. You want to be whole, content, loved, and successful in every area of your life. You don't want to fail; God wired you to win for you and for her. Take heart, if you are a follower of Christ, you have the Holy Spirit living in you. You also have the awesome ability to not only be transformed and sanctified but to reflect His glory to a world that desperately aches for it.

I also believe with all my heart most women really want to get this right. You want to be whole, content, loved, and effective in every area of your life. You don't want to leave anything undone; God wired you to have an influential voice. Take heart, if you are a follower of Christ, you have the Holy Spirit living in you. You have the awesome privilege of reflecting the emotional, sensitive, creative part of Father God, and you, too, get to reflect His glory.

Both sides of the zipper can work perfectly together when they choose to yield to the Holy Spirit and lay down the need to completely understand, be in control, always win, or be right. When the zipper is working well, there is nothing more wonderful! And when the zipper has gotten off track a bit, there is nothing more frustrating.

If you are wondering how to make meaningful changes so that you can experience a perfectly working zipper and operate according to God's original design, I have good news for you. In the next six chapters, I will reveal a list of transforming principles that may open your eyes and bring clarity. These proven principles have helped people of all ages experience fulfillment and transformation in their relationships. I call these principles "the keys."

They are:

Key #1: CAPTIVATE

Key #2: CULTIVATE

Key #3: COMMUNICATE

The following chapters will explain each of the keys for men and for women, with practical details to support each key. As you read through them, realize that heartfelt transformation requires a moment-by-moment decision to stop and ask, "God, what do *You* want to say to me about myself and both genders? What do *You* want to change in me? What do *You* want to say to me about *You*?"

Notice that questions concerning our identity are never focused on us and are always centered on the One who made us.

KEY #1 FOR MEN: CAPTIVATE

What captivates males and causes them to desire relationships with females?

Ladies, if you will open your hearts, you will see how remarkable men are. They are a gift to you, and you were not designed to live without them. Understanding these concepts has changed the relationships with various men in my life and created an atmosphere of trust, honor, and respect between us. They were created to be kings who know they need queens.

And gentlemen, if the women in your life do not honor you for your masculine traits, take time to get alone with God and ask Him to show you how women see you and how you see women. Pause, ponder, pray, and obey what the Lord reveals to you about yourself. God will give you the discernment to know when and how to battle for your family and the women in your life. Will you have the courage to step up and into your masculinity to protect and nurture the females in your world? Are you ready and willing to courageously claim your God-give identity so they can confidently take theirs? The rest of this chapter will show you how.

The keys for men transcend generations, which means that there is no age limit. They apply to males as young as two and as seasoned as 102. Also, they transcend connections, which means that they are not limited to one type of relationship, and they aren't just from women to men. For instance, in a family, the keys work from a wife toward a husband, from a father toward a son, from an aunt toward a nephew, from a brother toward a brother, and so on. In a work environment, the keys help women relate to men, and they help men relate to men. The same goes for friendships. The critical factor of the keys for men is that the *recipient* of the key is ... a man.

My hope is this section of the book will not only help men get a better understanding of who they are meant to be, but also help women see men through new lenses. As you incorporate the keys, I encourage you to notice (and take field notes on) how they are proving true in your life and in the lives of the people around you. I'm sure you'll agree it's fascinating. You'll get the most out of this transformative experience when you treat it like an "experiment," bringing your field notes to the Lord and asking Him to help you understand deep spiritual truths about yourself and others.

Because what I am about to share is so powerful, I have two warnings:

1. These keys may seem simple, but they are potent to open a man's heart so it's important to handle them with care. Men value honor and are born to give it and expect it in return. Therefore, if you try to manipulate them with false honor, they will recognize it (even if subconsciously), and it will backfire. Examine your motives and be sincere. It will do great damage to a man's heart and to your relationship with him if you manipulate. Take time to pray before you begin using a Key of Truth, and ask the Lord for a pure heart when you do so. Partnering with the Lord brings benefits to both you and the men in your life.

2. I want to be clear, once again, that these keys fit emotionally healthy men, not a man who demonstrates the traits of Narcissistic Personality Disorder. There seems to be an epidemic of this in our culture today. If you wonder if NPD could be true of you or a person in your life, seek professional help before moving forward.

The definition of *captivated* in the Merriam-Webster dictionary is "having one's interest or attention held or captured by something or someone charming, beautiful, entertaining, etc." Everything that's meaningful in life begins with interest and attention and moves us toward a relational connection.

As I said previously, most of the concepts I will introduce in this book apply across all relationships. However, this key refers to the way a man's interest and attention is uniquely captivated by a woman. Even so, please do not let your imagination default to the idea of physical attraction alone. A woman can captivate a man's interest and attention in many ways apart from sexuality. Certainly, a man should be captivated by his wife, but he can also value other women in appropriate ways.

The things that hold a man's interest and attention usually include honor and can be different from the things that hold a woman's. They often aren't the stereotypical female attributes portrayed in television and movies.

• Males crave partnership and need to be part of a team.

Men were built with a "team gene," and enjoy being on a team with men, but they also need to partner with women at almost every age and stage of their lives. They want trustworthy partners who enjoy being a part of their team. This partnership with females is designed to multiply love, gratitude, respect, and security for both genders.

Conversely, when a female continually competes with a male, he begins to view her as a friend and opponent, not someone who desires his provision, protection, and partnership. Overly competitive women emasculate men, and when a man feels emasculated, his energy drains and, over time, he will cease to provide and protect. Eventually, he gives up.

Women can allow men to win for them on a team. This is particularly fun when playing games. I love playing cornhole (or beanbag toss) with my family, especially when I can partner with Don, my son, Jonathan, or my son-in-law, Jon. When we are on the same team, we immediately bond because they feel they are winning for me (and they usually are).

Men, your score is not as important as her heart. It can be dangerous when men bring a winning mentality into the emotional part of a relationship because it can cause resentment and damage to a woman's heart. Sometimes winning or being right is everything to a man, but can cause insecurity in a female. Gentlemen, be careful. Because of your physical strength and size, this attitude can be threatening and will create distrust and fear to bubble up in her female soul.

God asks us to pause (take a moment, respond, and stop reacting), ponder (think about what God's Word says), pray (ask the Lord what He has to say about it), and then obey (do whatever He says). As we lay down our agendas and partner with each other, the more we will see God move in our hearts and sanctify us. This is how we team up with the Creator of the Universe. The truth is, He desires for men and women to be reconciled to one another and one in Christ (Galatians 3:28). When that happens, the results can be miraculous.

• Males live by an unspoken code of honor.

Have you ever noticed that boys and men tend to live by an unwritten honor code? It may be unspoken but if you ask a man, it is very real. Men are hard-wired to honor one another. They don't talk bad about other men unless they have to. Maybe the "team gene" in men brings an adherence to the honor code because of their need for survival, hunting, and battlefield brotherhood. Even with the gender lines more blurred than ever before, the honor code still remains intact for most men.

- **Males enjoy females who are fun and have a sense of humor.**

Many times a man is attracted to a woman because of how much fun they have together. Men thrive in recreational environments, not just with other men, but with women, too. Our culture says men like to laugh *at* women, but the truth is they love to laugh *with* women.

A guy likes a girl who has a playful attitude, gets his jokes, and knows how to laugh with him (and sometimes at herself). Women with a sense of humor make the adventure of life more valuable and exciting. They create joy instead of heaviness.

- **Males notice a female's authentic smile.**

A genuine smile from a woman can light up a man's world. Contrary to popular belief, men are interested in more than seductive smiles from women. Movies and television shows have convinced us that the only attraction men and women experience is sexual, but this is far from true. The kind of smile that captivates a good, respectable man is the kind that says, "I am emotionally healthy and balanced. I know who I am, and I enjoy life."

If a woman smiles in a man's presence, he perceives that she is happy. This encourages men in relationship with her because he knows he is doing a good job of caring for her. He can tell he has her approval, and he will more than likely continue to try to make her happy.

- **Males are captivated by females who are feminine and confident.**

Men enjoy women who embrace their femininity. They desire authentic friendship with women. A poised partner and self-assured teammate makes a man look and feel successful. Healthy men don't appreciate needy women or women who act like "silly girls." Men like women who know who they are.

A confident woman is pleasant, supportive, and understands her true identity. She recognizes her strengths and acknowledges her position as an individual and as a partner. A woman is radiant when she offers respect and desires partnership with the man who covers her. If a woman won't let a man do things for her, or if she is demanding, bossy, or overly assertive, he will probably find her unattractive. Nothing makes a man feel more masculine than a confident woman who wants to be on his team in life.

In a wife, a man is looking for a queen to be an equal partner with him, one who isn't independent. When men think women don't want or need their provision or protection, they can become more competitive. They feel emasculated and lean toward needing to prove their strength in some way. Most women don't understand that men fear not being enough for them. Therefore, when a female acts masculine, pointing out that she can provide for herself and protect herself, it doesn't bring out the best in a man. This has nothing to do with monetary compensation or physical size. It is about an attitude.

The topic of provision and protection inevitably leads me to single women. I can't count the number of times I have heard mothers mention that they have unmarried adult daughters who frequently express their loneliness and deep desire to be in a serious, committed relationship or married. As I've taught the keys to audience after audience, men have agreed that they view fiercely independent women as unappealing. This does not mean that they want women who are weak. Men do appreciate feminine strength. However, they may pull away from women who come across as headstrong, self-sufficient, and masculine.

Women often fail to understand that they can be both strong *and* feminine. This results in a quality I like to think of as *heartstrong*. It is a beautiful characteristic that attracts real men. Men who are self-assured and masculine realize that women complete what they lack. Males inherently recognize their need for femininity and will pursue it. But some women mistakenly believe that men desire women who can hold their own. Men are actually looking for heartstrong, feminine women. They prefer females who genuinely want them to provide for, protect, and lead them with their God-given masculinity. This posture is God's design and infuses females with the sense of security they were created to need.

In some ways, this truth can feel frustrating to a single woman who has no choice but to be the sole provider for herself (and/

or her children). What can she do? Should she stop displaying the determination required to provide for her household? Not at all.

She simply needs to be aware of her ability to adapt into something that will be hard on her out of necessity. Just the awareness of this possibility can empower her to ask for help, and that support can change everything. By taking her situation to the Lord, He will help her remain feminine. She cultivates a feminine attitude when she communicates to men, "I can do what I need to do," instead of "I can do anything, and I don't need you."

- **Males need females to bring emotional and physical color into their black-and-white worlds.**

Men can be concrete in their thinking and in the way they view life. They are decisive and practical; there is very little gray area. Males are built for battle and can strategize and make factual decisions without getting caught up in emotions. Yet they innately know they need women because females bring emotional color into their black-and-white worlds. Men are captivated by women because they are fascinating and mysterious, with a spontaneity that offers beauty, movement, fragrance, and texture. Deep inside, men appreciate that women bring soft stability and keep a man's wild sense of adventure grounded and balanced. The atmosphere she creates by her feminine presence is transformational for him.

When our son Jonathan moved back to Texas and built a new home as a bachelor, it had a distinctly masculine atmosphere. Missing his former home in Los Angeles, he proudly hung one of his surf boards above the kitchen cabinets. Jonathan is extremely creative and has the ability to decorate well, but his bachelor pad definitely lacked a feminine touch. Later, when he brought home his new bride, Laura, she embraced his love of surfing. But she also added floral soap, hand towels, and tissue boxes in every bathroom. There are comfortable pillows tucked into the corners of the couch, and scented candles that fill the whole house with a sweet aroma. It's no longer a bachelor pad; it's a warm and inviting home.

6

KEY #2 FOR MEN: CULTIVATE

How do females cultivate healthy connections with the
males in their world?

Typically, we think of the word "cultivate" in relation to farming or gardening. But the alternate definition of "fostering growth" can apply to the human heart. God desires us to honor Him by pursuing growth in all areas of their lives. Ideally, we will help one another grow by creating safe conditions for mental and emotional health.

How can we do so?

The more we study the innate needs of a man's heart, the more we can understand his unique needs. This usually requires only small tweaks. A dedication to deliberate lovingkindness will cultivate a man's soul. We can help him develop into who he was always meant to be.

Remember, our intent in the beginning is simply to do it for the Lord and trust Him with the outcome.

- **Males are wired to lead, not dominate.**

Cultivating leadership in men causes confidence and growth in a humble and teachable man. God wants men to lead and shepherd His way. In every organization, including families, there must be a leader, not a dominator. A leader serves, guides, and shows the way while a dominator seeks to have control. A man who leads by domination will eventually create fear and resentment and cause a woman to shut down. Jesus modeled leadership by shepherding with a perfect balance of humility, authority, tenderness, and strength. This type of leadership causes those in a man's care to rest and grow under his covering.

- **Males usually work with success in mind.**

Men prefer to focus on doing, not just trying. Because they are warriors, hunters, and kings they must see the potential for success before they try something new. For example, if a hunter is hunting for food, he needs to make sure his shot can effectively hit the target, or he might become the food himself. When a man goes into battle, he has to believe he will be the victor, or he already feels defeated. When men don't see a strong possibility for success, they usually won't begin.

This is also true for men in relationships. God wired men to war and win as individuals and as teammates. A man needs to feel he will attain success in her eyes, or he will not continue. A female's attitude and gratitude toward a man will make or break his desire to provide for and protect her.

- **Males connect with females who give them space to try and learn new things.**

Men need opportunities to learn how to do new things. He needs to assert his masculinity by figuring out problems himself. In other words, if you ask him to do something, then stand over him, telling him how he should do it, he'll cease to try. This goes for mowing the lawn, loading the dishwasher, driving the car, planning dates, scheduling vacations, or anything. This is also true in the workplace when it comes to planning a presentation or preparing for a meeting. Women must give them space, grace, and the opportunity to try and learn.

I can remember the first time I saw this in Jonathan when he was two years old. We were out in the driveway, and he was trying to learn how to ride his new trike. He was pushing down on both pedals with equal force at the same time and, of course, going nowhere fast. He was getting furious and starting to cry.

I bent down beside him and tried to help him by pressing just one foot and saying, "One foot at a time."

He would get more frustrated and say, "Mom, I do it myself!"

I still remember wondering why something so insignificant was making him so angry at me. Don walked out of the garage and told me Jonathan needed to figure it out on his own, which he eventually did. But the mom in me found it hard to watch.

About six years later, we were at the lake, and Don and I were in a boat anchored to a buoy in a cove. Jonathan and Holly were in a canoe, and the current began to cause them to drift away from us. Jonathan was about eight years old and had not yet learned how to paddle using oars. Don stood and watched for a while, as Jonathan got angrier by the minute. They repeatedly went around and around in circles, while Holly sat and enjoyed the view. I wanted Don to jump in, swim over, and help him, but Don calmly yelled out one or two instructions to Jonathan. Then he turned to me and said, "He'll figure it out, just give him time." Don knew Jonathan needed to figure it out on his own. And you know what? He eventually did.

- **Males need transition time.**

Because men are single-focused, they need time to transition from one location to another. It may take from 15 to 30 minutes, depending on how long he has been in the other place mentally or physically. For example, when a man goes from a day of work to an evening with his wife (and kids), he needs time to adjust. It's respectful to him when a woman realizes this and responds accordingly.

Men have a pattern of transitioning at the end of the day, and often it will be the same way, in the same order, for the same amount of time. Think of it like this: When a man comes home, he may greet his wife and family, but he is not completely "home" yet. He may stop at the mailbox, sort the mail, go to the restroom, wash his face, change his clothes, and then come in to engage with the family. Until he goes through this process, he cannot offer his undivided attention. It's helpful when a woman greets him but doesn't immediately ask questions or try to give him details about her day. He may not be emotionally available, just yet. After he's made the transition to being home, he can fully connect and engage.

One of the best gifts that a wife can give her husband is to train their children to honor his transition time. Imagine a loving father returning after a challenging day of work, only to be tackled by kids who are excited to see him but are also excited to ask him to fix a toy, to give permission to buy a video game, to help with homework, to play catch in the backyard, to hear what the teacher said, and so on. It's just too much, too soon and can trigger his frustration. If kids are taught to let their father have a moment to breathe when he gets home, they will experience far greater warmth and receptivity to their requests later.

What about women who work outside the home? Women are highly adaptable—a key we will discuss soon—but most jobs require them to face a constant barrage of questions, issues, challenges, and problems to be solved. Therefore, they may need the same consideration and adjustment period when they get home at the end of the day. If you're married, and you both work full-time, study each other and find a way to transition that works for both of you. The point of transition time is to shift from the harshness of the outside world to the softness of your safe place at home.

I wish I had known this years ago. It would have helped Don and me so much, especially when our kids were young. I would have been more considerate toward him and would have shown him more respect in this area. Being a stay-at-home mom often meant I was starving for adult conversation so when Don came home, I would immediately bombard him with all the things I had experienced throughout the day.

But he would walk in the door with his mind elsewhere. Because he talked on the phone all day long, the last thing he wanted to do was answer a bunch of questions. He just wanted to be quiet. Eventually, the Lord led me to start allowing Don to have transition time. After I learned to wait a while, Don no longer resisted talking to me, and I no longer feared approaching him. I knew he would be ready to connect with me after he had a few moments to adapt. To pour out the contents of my heart immediately after he got home caused him to feel overloaded; it was difficult for him to shift quickly. Allowing him to have time to adjust kept my feelings from getting hurt whenever he seemed to be disinterested and detached.

- **Males need hobbies and physical outlets.**

Some men enjoy golf. Others enjoy woodworking or attending car shows. For some it's fishing, hunting, playing basketball with friends, or tending land in the country. For most men, these outlets and hobbies fulfill their need for competition and adventure.

There are times men may invite women to be a part of an outing, but sometimes they just want time with other guys or time alone. If a man does invite a female to join him, what he is most interested in is her presence. During these adventures, most men don't want conversation; they simply desire "shoulder to shoulder" companionship with her. It seems strange to women, but men feel very connected and content when sitting silently shoulder to shoulder with people who are important to them. During these times, men just want to relax and not have to provide for or protect anyone.

An example is when my friend's husband invited her to go deer hunting with him. She decided she would "gift" her husband with her presence. Being a "girly girl," she knew it would be a big sacrifice, but she was thrilled he invited her into his space and was anxious to prove her love for her man by going with him. When the day came, they rose early, loaded into his pickup truck, and traveled out into the woods to get positioned in the deer blind. They sat silently for hours, which seemed like weeks to her. Periodically, she would glance over at her husband's face. He was obviously content sitting there in total silence—he had his woman and was ready to prove his hunting skill to her. He looked like he was in heaven! As minutes turned into hours, he stayed content and happy, while she grew cold, stiff, uncomfortable, and more miserable by the moment. All she kept thinking was, *If we could just talk, our time together would be so much more fun and fulfilling.*

On their way home after an entire day of hunting, he reached over, grabbed her hand, and said, "Thank you so much for coming with me. That was one of the best days I've had with you in a long time!"

She thought, *Oh Lord, please don't ever let him ask me again! That silence was awful!*

My friend was glad she went, but only because her husband was thrilled. He loved being in a deer blind, shoulder-to-shoulder, however, it was a sacrifice for her. She was cultivating the ideal conditions for him, and his mental and emotional health were able to thrive.

A Brief Warning for Men: As with all of life, a balance of hobbies and physical outings is important. However, when your own interests become your primary focus, it feels like rejection to the important women in your life. Look for ways to cultivate fun things that you can do together.

Submission works wonders when it is mutual.

KEY #3 FOR MEN: COMMUNICATE

How can females communicate with the males
in their lives to connect and gain trust?

The first two keys—Captivate and Cultivate—set the stage for the most important key of all. What good is captivating a man's interest and attention if you don't know how to communicate with him?

Both men and women alike who desire to have healthy relationships need to learn how to facilitate good communication. It is essential, but few of us understand how to do it. The rest of this chapter will help you.

- **Males need verbal appreciation.**

Expressing verbal appreciation to a man—both privately and publicly—causes his strengths to multiply. When people choose to be vulnerable and voice things they like and respect about the men in their lives, it puts wind in their sails and liquid gold in their cups. Two of the most powerful words to a man are simply "thank you." This seems basic, but it is remarkably potent. When friends and colleagues target specific behaviors in men by expressing gratitude through words, attitudes, and actions, oftentimes those excellent behaviors increase. A man loves to know when he's doing something right, and he measures his success by the contentment of those around him, especially women. Men want to protect women who express appreciation for what they provide. A heartfelt "thank you" tells him that he has delivered on what he was responsible for.

I never realized how important my words of gratitude were to Don until I began to encourage him with intentional words of thankfulness. As soon as I did, he began to trust me more and more. It didn't happen quickly. It took a while for him to believe I was sincere because it was so foreign to him. I had withheld genuine appreciation for so long that he wondered what I was up to.

We all need encouragement; men need it as much as women do. What can this look like?

DIRECTLY—WE MIGHT SAY *TO* A MAN:

- You're doing a great job!
- Thank you for being considerate of other's opinions.
- I appreciate you for looking for ways to help and support us all.
- People notice your integrity and character.

INDIRECTLY – WHEN TALKING WITH OTHERS, WE MIGHT REMARK *ABOUT* A MAN:

- He is wise, and operates in truth with integrity.

- He does so much for us, and I am grateful for so many things about him.

- He is very good at what he does. Many people respect him in his field.

- He is a great dad!

- He is an example of a godly man.

Ask the Lord to show you the strengths in the men around you and give you the courage to voice it.

• Males appreciate authentic hero language.

Males of all ages and cultures understand and appreciate "hero language." It encourages a man's masculinity and makes him feel wise and strong, suggesting he is capable and has what it takes.

Although it may seem similar to verbal appreciation, it is different. Verbal appreciation acknowledges what he has done. Hero language acknowledges what he can do.

When we use hero language with a man, it speaks life into him, reminding him that we trust him to do the right thing for our team. It builds confidence and leadership in his heart. Hero language can come from both men and women, but it is particularly potent when it comes from females, young and old. Men want to provide, and women need to let them use their masculinity to show their strength.

The next time you observe young children with their dads, uncles, or grandfathers, you will more than likely see the hero and the child who feels safe with him.

EXAMPLES OF HERO LANGUAGE:

- Can you help me _____?
- I need you.
- You are the only one who can _____.
- Wow, you really saved the day!
- We wouldn't be the same without you.
- You make me happy when you _____.
- You make the right decisions.
- You will know what to do.
- I know you've got it.
- When you lead like that, I feel safe.
- Thank you for looking out for me.

Get the idea? It is not a specific or exact phrase but an attitude of trust and assurance.

- **Males respond well to communication bullet points during conversation.**

Men care about the bottom line, and sometimes women have a tendency to go into a lot of detail when talking. This can cause men to lose focus and tune out. A man feels tortured when a woman goes on and on without a point. It's easier for men to focus when women use "bullet points" to begin a conversation. Men are wired to provide, therefore, if a woman is clear and to the point about what she needs from him, he will usually try hard to provide it for her. Ladies, men want to listen longer if you let him know what to expect. For example, you might say, "When you have a moment, I have three things to talk to you about ...."

This is good for women in the workplace to remember this as they communicate with their male co-workers, supervisors, and employees. It's important to be concise and clear in meetings, emails, and conversations with men. Men can't absorb all the details until they know the bullet points and why the details matter.

It's also important to remember that men like to know the main issue or point. Before you open your mouth, ask yourself, "What is the main thing here?" If there is no main thing, be sure to tell him that all you need him to do is listen. Ask him if he would be willing to "hold the handle of your pitcher" as you pour out what you collected throughout the day. It is a huge gift to a man when a woman lets him know in advance if she wants him to "fix" or simply let her share.

So what is *my* point here? Being considerate of the way he thinks will help him hear what you want him to know.

- **Males appreciate females who invite conversation rather than insist on it.**

Men are like telescopes; if they're interrupted, they lose their amazing ability to focus. It's helpful when others give men time to think and an opportunity to respond. When a woman asks a question, she often feels ignored or frustrated when a man doesn't answer quickly. A man is wired to focus on one thing at a time so he needs a moment to shift his focus from the first task or conversation to the next. Men typically say what they mean and mean what they say. They need time to think and choose their words carefully. I see this often when coaching men and women.

Imagine that the husband is watching a football game. Something about the family's weekend plans pops into his wife's mind (because her radar is always on). She immediately turns to him and asks him a relevant question about the family schedule. Her husband keeps looking at the television screen and doesn't respond. She asks him again, this time feeling frustrated because she has ten other things beeping on her "radar."

"Hold on just a minute," he says, still watching the game. His wife feels ignored and tries again.

You probably know what happens next. A relaxing afternoon takes a turn, and an argument erupts out of nowhere. The woman is hurt, and the man doesn't even know what happened.

How could this scene be improved?

Rewind the moment and play it again. A husband is watching a football game. But this time, when something about the family's weekend plans pops into his wife's mind, she honors her husband's focus by waiting for a commercial before bringing up anything significant. Then, during the break, she mentions the scheduling conflict without frustration like this:

"I would like your attention for about five minutes. Let me know when you can give me your attention. There are three bullet points about our weekend plans that you may not know. I am not upset about anything, I just need your input."

Think it sounds too easy? Does it seem awkward or scripted? Just try it. This approach will be a game-changer for your communication.

Here are the five core elements that make it effective.

1. She waits for a break in his focus (the commercial).
2. She asks for a specific amount of time (five minutes).
3. She invites *him* to choose the best time to talk (honor and respect).
4. She lets him know how many bullet points there will be, as well as the main issue (three bullet points, the weekend plans).
5. She lets him know that the dialogue will not be emotionally taxing for him ("I am not upset ...").

This approach is an invitation to partner for the benefit of the entire family, and it allows his focus to catch up with where her mind already is.

I hope you can easily apply this model sentence to a circumstance that is not a husband and wife, as well. A man who is focused on a project at work can receive the same type of language. You can use the model with its five core elements in any conversation with a male.

For instance, someone communicating with a male colleague in the workplace might say:

"I would like your attention for about fifteen minutes when it is a good time for you. There are two quick bullet points about our next client meeting that you may not already know. I just need your input."

It also works well when emailing or texting. You can adjust these five core elements to fit a conversation with your son, brother, father, or anyone.

- **Males need females to give them time to speak without interrupting.**

Men process differently than women and are usually more apt to trust facts than feelings. When they're processing or taking a moment to think before speaking, it's because they're accessing information. Because males are wired to hunt, it may take them a while to "find their feelings" and communicate them exactly as they intend. Some men are more closed than others because of their backgrounds or upbringings. But almost all men need time to process what they're feeling and courageously bring it into the light. In other words, when men are asked something that requires an emotion, they usually need time to express it. If it takes too long, some women feel a need to tell men what they are feeling because emotions are much easier to access and express for females. I used to be a master at this. I honestly thought I was helping the men in my life, but in reality, I was handicapping them and making them feel emasculated. If men want help, they will ask for it. Most of the time, they don't need anyone to help them communicate, they just need time. There is nothing wrong with asking questions, but men don't like a lot of them, and they don't like to be interrupted. Interruptions often frustrate men and backfire on women.

Women usually beg men to express their emotions because that's how women connect.

But men do not connect like women do. Rather than reveal their emotions immediately, men tend to strategically conceal them until the right moment. (God may have included this tendency in their hunter and warrior mentality). Instead of expecting a man to hurry up and share how he feels, ask God for the patience and grace to wait for his words of wisdom. His wisdom has a different perspective than yours. A man of honor will never say something just to fill the silence. He will consider every word until he is sure that what he is saying feels true. He strives to support his feelings with facts, not emotions. That takes masculine courage, and when he finally speaks, it will be worth the wait.

There are two types of interrupting that may occur when a man takes his time to respond.

We all know how rude it can be to interrupt someone's words. However, it might also be inconsiderate to interrupt someone's silence.

One time, I was coaching a couple and noticed that the wife often expressed an impatient attitude when her husband took a long time to answer my questions. After a minute of silence, she would tell him to hurry up and answer, or she would fill in his sentences and talk over him, putting her own words in his mouth. Men feel emasculated and may lash out in anger when women talk for them (and over them) by adding words.

Men respond well to respectful communication, and they do show emotions. They just do it in a very different way than women. They may not put words to their emotions quickly, but they do have ways of showing how they're feeling. They use nonverbal communication to express it. Sometimes when emotions are extreme, it's through grunts and sounds. Other times they express emotions through their upper bodies, using their chest, arms, and hands. For example, when a group of men are watching or playing sports, they use high fives, chest bumps, or even a hearty shove. Men may hug, but they usually include a strong slap on the back as a way to release the energy and emotion they're feeling.

- **Males want females to communicate what they need or desire with respect.**

Men don't like to guess what people need or desire. In fact, it feels cruel to men when others don't tell them what they want. How can he provide what he doesn't know is needed or desired? It feels like a guessing game, set up for him to lose. It's especially frustrating to play the guessing game with women because men and women think so differently. Men feel defeated because they know they rarely guess correctly. Remember, they don't like engaging in something they don't think they can accomplish.

Ladies, be courageous enough to start sharing your desires and needs. You are setting them up for success. I know it can be scary, but it changed my relationships with the males in my life, even my grandsons.

When you respectfully ask men for what you need or desire, it sets them up to win. Ask kindly, without an entitled attitude. It makes it easier for him to give you what you need as a gift instead of a requirement.

There are women who falsely believe it is selfish to ask me for anything. But to men, it is selfish not to ask. It's frustrating to them. I personally believe this lie has greatly affected the Body of Christ. Women need to learn to see men as the strong providers they were made to be and help them succeed. They can do this by respectfully communicating their needs and desires so the men can feel good about providing it.

Providing for females builds healthy masculinity in males. I've heard men say, "If she will just tell me what she wants, I want to provide it for her. But I can't read her mind!"

For years, I believed I was being selfless when I would not ask Don for anything. I thought I should be quiet and pray, and God would do the rest. Believing this lie created a lot of disappointment, frustration, and distance for both of us, which led to bitterness in my heart toward my husband. I was expecting Don to know my expectations, which was so unfair to him. He can't think like a female, even if he tried! Like many women, I did not fully understand what God meant by submission so I willed myself to be quiet, which caused me to grow resentful.

It wasn't until I began expressing my desires to Don that I realized how much he really wanted to provide for me. I just needed to have the courage to be vulnerable and ask him for what I needed without fear of rejection. The results were shocking, and healing began when he believed I needed him. I am so thankful God loves to help us become better people and retrain us when we've gone off course.

The Bible encourages us to submit to one another (Ephesians 5:21). However, submission does not mean that you are silent and blindly follow a person. Submission means that you follow God's design, plan, and order. When we submit to one another, we honor God with a respectful, equal partnership because we were designed to take our positions and thrive there.

- **Males are highly sensitive to disrespect and eventually become defensive when they feel repeatedly disrespected.**

When men are disrespected, it often makes them feel threatened, and the warrior, hunter, and king in them comes out swinging, emotionally or verbally. It's part of a man's DNA to be a provider and protector, so when that gets undermined, he can go into self-protection mode by distancing, disconnecting, and dishonoring others. When he feels disrespected, he'll begin to show frustration and an attitude that signals his displeasure. When a woman disrespects a man, he wonders if she thinks he is stupid and incapable of protecting her and providing for her needs and/or the needs of the family.

Ladies, it's selfless and courageous of you to ask him if you have done or said something that made him feel emasculated. Throughout our marriage, I would offer suggestions to Don about things around the house, thinking I was helping him. He would immediately become frustrated and defensive. I know now that he perceived my "help" as my lack of confidence in him and his abilities. This was not my intention, but motive had nothing to do with what he was feeling. It was life changing for me when I began to understand more about what triggered the "warrior mode" in Don.

In unhealthy families, people treat children like spouses and spouses like children. While men like to be cared for and sometimes even nurtured, they don't like to be patronized or treated like a child. Mothering strips a man of his masculinity and cuts him to the core. This sometimes causes a man to shut down emotionally, and he will eventually stop trying to provide and protect. Many times women see potential in the men in their lives and want to encourage them; however, this encouragement can be perceived as "mothering." Ladies, ask your husbands, boyfriends, or co-workers to signal you kindly if they feel you are mothering them. If it has become a habit, or if you saw it in your family of origin, ask him to give you a subtle signal so that you can stop.

- **Males distance themselves from negative people who constantly criticize them.**

Men are hunters, warriors, and kings, and are highly sensitive to criticism. Some women believe criticism creates a desire to change because that's how most women are wired. Yet with men, it causes the opposite response. When men feel criticized, it feels emasculating, and they disconnect. Encouragement and praise bring about more change than criticism.

One of my girlfriends oversees a team that handles corporate communication. A man on her team had written something that contained incorrect information, and when she noticed it, she called to let him know. As she was explaining what needed to be changed, he snapped at her and hung up the phone before she could even say goodbye. Because she had been to one of our conferences, she realized she may have relayed the information in a way that sounded like criticism, which caused him to feel emasculated. That's why he shut down completely and hung up. The next day she took time to meet with him and talk about what happened. Sure enough, he confirmed she had made him feel stupid by the way she had handled his mistake. Her awareness of the keys helped her see the problem, correct it, and find a more beneficial way to communicate in the future.

There you have it. Your life will change when you Captivate, Cultivate, and Communicate with the men you know. Whether you are a man or a woman, you may want to read over these keys more than once, pausing to pray and listen to the Lord.

Because of our culture's recent confusion about male and female roles, many women may read this list and wonder where the strong, courageous men have gone. Men certainly are responsible for their own actions, yet I believe the cultural trends may have emasculated them to the point of dropping their warrior swords, suggesting they need to be more passive, emotional, and less masculine. When your core identity is labeled "toxic" by some, you tend to shy away from being who you really are.

At the same time, young women are confused and feel weak if they admit they want or need a man in their lives. Women instinctively know they need men, but it feels dangerous to let down our guards and trust them to provide for and protect us. In fact, I have known women who feel a sense of panic when they consider giving a man the responsibility they assume should be theirs alone.

A woman who drops her sword might begin thinking, *What if he doesn't step up to the challenge of fighting for me?* The worry is overwhelming. For a woman to cease self-protection requires a level of vulnerability that is a risk at best, and at worst, heartbreaking and disappointing.

Most of us know more than a few beautiful, talented, successful women who are battle-weary and yearn for true partnership with a godly man. Some of these women believe that they must be strong and independent in order for men to desire them. Because of our culture, others fear that without a shield of strength, men will use and abuse them. Sadly, this is the very mindset many men find off-putting. Why would a man be attracted to women who communicate with their words or attitude that they don't need him? God wired men to magnetize toward confident, smart, balanced women who want to partner with them. Emotionally healthy men know in order to walk in their identity, they need a woman who can walk in hers. It builds courage in a man to be around a woman who allows him to fulfill his God-ordained role, successfully care for her, and support her as she fulfills her own.

Ladies, if you are having trouble getting men to see you as a valuable partner, spend time alone with God and ask Him to show you how men see you and how you see men. Then pause, ponder, pray, and obey what the Lord reveals to you one step at a time. The first hurdle is trusting God to help you do it His way. Even if you don't always know or understand the ending, He is trustworthy and only wants what is best for you.

The work begins with willingness. Will you highlight the best things about the men in your life? Will you trust that God wired them to provide for and protect you? Will you believe real men want someone to fight for?

Will you believe that someone just might be you?

TESTIMONIALS FROM MEN

For anyone grappling with the pain of a lost marriage or the chaos of a strained one, this is a guide to rediscovering God's intent for marriage. The call to personal responsibility and growth resonated deeply. Cristie invites you to reflect on your own actions and beliefs, offering a fresh vision of what God can do when we align with His purposes. Since implementing the keys, I have worked to rebuild a wrecked marriage, and God has restored the family I once took for granted. Thank you, Cristie, for your faithfulness in acting on God's prompting.

Matthew B.

Understanding the keys showed me ways to step into my God-given identity as a man. The Bible is full of stories that show the roles God has given man and woman. Nothing has changed since that time, God still creates men to lead. Reading these keys helped remind me how simple these truths are. It also gave me a framework to be able to better communicate with women at work. Our culture has tried to twist these truths so it is very refreshing to read something that calls out who we were created to be with a biblical worldview.

Matthew H.

These truths have not only given me a deeper understanding of myself, but also of everyone around me. I was once ignorant enough to think I would never understand the female mind, but these keys have radically transformed the way I relate to and interact with people of the opposite sex. After reading this book, I feel seen and heard! It's like the author had an x-ray into my mind. It has helped me immensely in all of my day-to-day relationships.

Brandon M.

Joan and I started practicing the keys together, which we highly recommend doing! We were reminded that we are fearfully and wonderfully made by the very hand of God. He made us man and woman, as compliments to each other. He knew we needed each other. A genuine, sold out love for Jesus and a relationship rooted in love and respect for each other are essential to forging a strong marriage, just as God intended.

Tom C.

The keys have provided some new insight and healthy conversations with my wife of over forty years. Who would have thought I might be unaware of some of those truths? The most significant truth for me is stated as, "Females are designed with a protective fear factor." I am grateful for that understanding and the mindset I now have regarding my desire to make certain my wife feels safe and secure.

Sonny Gann, MA, LPC
Trellis Christian Counseling, LLC

The keys have been a transforming guide in both my personal and professional life. These insights have deepened my empathy, sharpened my leadership skills, and helped me better navigate relationships with my wife, family members, colleagues, and friends. I highly recommend them to everyone who wants a greater understanding and guidance for successful male and female relationships.

Randy H.

KEY #1 FOR WOMEN: CAPTIVATE

What captivates females and causes them
to desire relationships with males?

Most women today are exhausted, lonely, and deeply desire to drop their swords, remove their dented battle gear, and be figuratively (and literally) held by a man who thinks she is worth fighting for. He may be her father, boyfriend, friend, brother, husband or supervisor, but when he provides for and protects her within the limits of a particular role, he is offering a "covering" she is designed to to need. Women who appear domineering and rough on the outside are often girls who just want to know they are worth covering.

I have learned that most of these females have not yet experienced the provision and protection they were created to need. Many are afraid to lower their swords. God created men to be kings of their families and organizations. Kings need women to be queens.

The keys for women will empower men to courageously care for the females in their lives if females will allow them the privilege. These principles will also help women better understand themselves, their daughters, their mothers, and their friends.

Just as I cautioned you not to use the keys to manipulate the men in your life, I'm gently warning you not to use these keys to manipulate the women in your life. It's especially easy for a male to assert his masculinity to get females to do what he wants. She wants to please you because she knows she needs the security you bring. Take time to pray before you begin using one of the keys, and ask the Lord to purify your motives. Partnering with God benefits both you and the females of all ages in your life.

To deepen your understanding of these keys about women, remain curious. Observe others and take field notes as you notice how these keys prove true in so many specific ways.

Take your notes to the Lord during your times of prayer, and ask Him to teach you how to love women ferociously. God wants you to succeed even more than you do.

Females at every age and stage of life are captivated by men who model trustworthy strength because strength means security to her and those she loves.

- **Females are designed with a protective fear factor.**

Because females are more physically vulnerable, God may have wired them with a heightened sensitivity and awareness of danger. Initially, this idea may feel offensive to some women, but I have seen the "female fear factor" proven true time and time again. When I share about this concept in conferences, I start out by asking a simple question. First, I ask men to raise their hands if they've feared for their personal safety in the past month. Rarely do any hands go up. Then I ask women to raise their hands if they've feared for their personal safety in the past month. The majority of the women raise their hands. Then I ask if they've feared for their personal safety in the past week? Hands stay up. Yesterday? Hands are still in the air.

Looking over the audience, I can tell this shocks the men in the room. They had no idea that women are always on high alert when walking through an airport, shopping mall, or parking lot alone. It does not occur to a man to be afraid in the same situation. As warriors, hunters, and kings, men are not wired to feel fear as a first response. Men can calm the female fear factor by recognizing that women are wired to fear things he doesn't. When he is aware of this, it can benefit them both.

When a female perceives that something is a threat—even if it is not truly a threat—she will give a signal that her senses are on high alert. She may make an alarmed facial expression or blurt out a startled noise. She may put her hands up to her face or mouth. Her eyes may widen or squint. She may not always say she is fearful, but her face, voice, and body language will let you know, if you pay attention.

It is important to note that sometimes a woman's fear surfaces when someone she cares about is doing something she perceives as dangerous, such as hunting or riding a motorcycle. This "fear language" manifests itself through questions.

EXAMPLES OF A WOMAN'S FEAR LANGUAGE:

- Are you okay?

- Is it safe?

- Please be careful!

- Do you know what you are doing?

- Is this safe for the kids?

- Are you sure?

- Can we afford this?

The hunter, warrior, and king that is built into men often mistakes these questions as evidence that a woman is thinking they're inadequate or stupid. Males may assume that she is doubting *them*. That triggers determination in him to forge ahead, which exacerbates her fear. Subconsciously, she recognizes that she has given you the right to provide for and protect her. When you participate in an activity or behavior she sees as risky, she may be wondering what life would be like if something happened to you. If you were gone, who would take care of everything? She needs you, and she knows it. So if you did something to trigger her fear, don't ignore it or blame it on her. There is great power when a man learns how to offer his strength to make a woman feel safe. The next time you notice her using "fear language" and asking a lot of questions, calmly reassure her that you have already thought through those questions, and she is safe.

This applies far beyond the marriage relationship. Sisters can feel afraid when brothers are driving too fast. Aunts can feel afraid when nephews are standing too close to a ledge.

Mothers can feel afraid when sons make quick decisions. Female friends can feel afraid when male friends engage in adventure travel or abruptly quit their jobs. Women in the workplace can feel afraid when male colleagues take calculated risks with high stakes projects.

When you observe the phenomenon of a woman's fear language long enough, you will notice that these scenarios are not instigated by men. Even women can make other women feel afraid. But Christian women know they're not supposed to be fearful. As a woman increases her trust in the Lord, her fear decreases dramatically. She becomes more sanctified, and less and less anxious when a godly man reassures her along the way.

- **Females are wired to seek heroes from a young age and never outgrow it.**

A woman without a leader feels exposed. Women need to have heroes as much as the men in their lives need to be heroes. God designed women to desire the traits that men were designed to display: strength, confidence, tenderness, trustworthiness, and heroic leadership. A true hero brings a sense of safety to an entire family or organization. Safety is captivating to a woman. In fact, a woman is so driven by her God-designed need for a hero, that if a man does not provide a sense of safety for her, she will find a hero in someone else, even if she has to become the hero herself!

A leader's best role model is Jesus. If he longs to lead like Jesus, the Holy Spirit will partner with him and develop the hero within him at breakneck speed.

- **Females unconsciously monitor the contentment of significant males in their lives.**

For a woman, monitoring her environment begins very early in life. Even as a little girl, a female knows that the covering of a man makes her feel safe. Therefore, a woman will monitor a man who is important to her because she wants him to be happy with her. She believes if he's happy with her, he will provide for and protect her. She also subconsciously believes that if he is unhappy, it is probably because of her. She will try to please him so she can feel safe. To a male, monitoring may seem controlling, but a woman's need for protection drives her. Just knowing a man is pleased with her makes her feel more secure.

If a man ever wonders what a woman is thinking, she is almost always thinking, "Is he happy right now? Is he pleased with me?" Even when these thoughts are not actively occupying her thoughts, she maintains a subconscious awareness of his well-being (or lack thereof).

God wired women to be a helpmeet, and the desire to connect with a man at the intersection of his need and her ability to help is deeply satisfying to her.

- **Females are attracted to males who strike a balance of authority and humility.**

A man who operates with a balance of authority and humility makes women feel secure. When a man aligns himself with the Lord, his heart and attitudes change, and women begin to yield to his leadership with ease. A woman thrives in this type of environment; it allows her to become vulnerable, lay down her sword, and become who God created her to be. Conversely, women find it difficult to be vulnerable and submissive to prideful men who abuse authority. Women who know God's character understand that He "opposes the proud but gives grace to the humble" (James 4:6 NIV). Pride is a form of self-absorption. It is evident in someone who is not yielded to God and wants his or her own way. A prideful person thinks they know best and are always right. The sin of pride never affects just one person; it affects the entire family or organization. When a man humbles himself and partners with a woman, safety and security cover her heart. If men don't humble themselves, the

Lord will have no choice but to humble them Himself, and that can hurt everyone around him. This is often one of the greatest fears of females because her security is connected to him.

The greatest gift a man can give his family is to follow the example of Christ and lead as a kind shepherd and a responsible king. Healthy women recognize that submission is something they are wired by God to desire. Submitting is not scary but safe when a leader is walking with a balance of humility and authority. God designed submission to be an avenue of safety for both men and women. When a woman submits to authority, she sets an example for her daughters and builds courage in her sons. Likewise, how a man treats his wife and daughters models for his sons the value (or lack of value) he has for females. This is the same outside the home. In the workplace, how men behave toward women establishes an example to male employees and colleagues.

Even if you didn't have a Christ-like earthly father who has led you well, you have a Heavenly Father who's desperate to love you and show you the way of humility. Jesus is the perfect example of authority. Study His example in the Bible, then pray and ask Him to show you what He sees about your leadership style and what He wants you to speak over the women in your life to build them up and encourage them. Allow Him to strengthen and train you so you can become a godly leader who is captivating to those He has placed under your care.

- **Females need male partnership when raising children.**

Women need their children's fathers to be engaged in child rearing. When husbands are not partnering with their wives, the kids often take advantage of their mothers. The absence of a man can be the loneliest feeling in the world for women, especially during their child's adolescent years. Babies are physically demanding, but teens are emotionally demanding. During middle school and high school, adolescents can display a level of entitlement that emotionally drains their mom. If a dad is not present in ways that support her, the kids can deeply damage their mother's heart and cause her to lose confidence. Eventually, she may give up and give in to the kids, which can end in disaster.

Satan sets another trap for women, especially for those whose husbands are not present or emotionally connected. This creates the temptation for moms to become too enmeshed in their children's lives. Some women transfer their need to love and be loved to their kids. This can cause mothers to try to win approval and friendship by acting "cool." This is a critical mistake during the developmental years. If the individualization of the teen has not been allowed to flourish during their adolescent years, their growth will be stunted and boundaries may be hard to define. This will make it hard for the teen to individualize and build a life of his or her own, making personal growth, maturity, and marriage difficult.

The bottom line is, children have plenty of friends, but they only have one mom and one dad. We have to be parents to them until they are adults and no longer need parenting. If we have done our part well, they will grow up and respect us, choose to be our friends, and come to us when they need advice or counsel. It's a sweet reward for parenting God's way. Hard work and commitment are always an opportunity for great rewards.

KEY #2 FOR WOMEN: CULTIVATE

*How do males cultivate healthy relationships
with the females in their lives?*

The heart of a woman is like a garden. When the soil is fertile, many things can flourish and multiply. Therefore, it takes intentionality to cultivate her mental and emotional health. If you plant fear, doubt, frustration, or insecurity, the environment of her heart will grow and multiply pain and fear. It is wise to take opportunities to sow seeds of gratitude, patience, and appreciation into the females you care about. Doing your part allows God to do His, and His portion can bring supernatural benefits to you, your family, or organization.

- **Females are highly adaptable.**

One of a female's superpowers is adaptability. However, as usual, the enemy uses a person's greatest gifts as his most effective weapons against them. Current culture has somehow caused females to believe they are only validated when they can do what men do. Believing this subliminal lie will eventually destroy a female heart and make her body sick. Ladies, let's wake up!

Women can easily acclimate and step into any position that is left vacant. God knew women needed this kind of adaptability because in some cases, they might find themselves raising children alone. Maybe they are military wives or have husbands who travel for work. They may be single, divorced, or widowed. When a husband is absent, women adapt by taking the man's role, and they operate in survival mode. They will do whatever is necessary—fight, claw, and strategize—to provide for themselves and their children. This can cause burnout and depression in a woman who has been forced into taking a masculine stance.

My heart breaks for single mothers whose dreams and hearts have been shattered. They usually had no desire to end up where they are. They must grieve the loss of their dreams, yet continue to care for their babies while working outside the home. It is cruel and breaks my heart. Satan seems to work overtime to make them feel incomplete, guilty, and overextended. He wants them to work so hard and become so busy that they don't have much time to care for themselves, talk with God, read His Word, or go to church. The enemy lies to single mothers, trying to convince them they don't have time for themselves or their friends. He knows what encourages and strengthens them, and he tries to keep them away from those things. Often, she has no energy to fight off the devil, she is just trying to exist.

While a woman's adaptability is powerful as she thrives in different seasons, the truth is she wasn't physically or emotionally built to carry what a man carries every day. Her superpowers are very different from his.

• **Females are designed to bring forth life and beauty.**

God gave women the ability to conceive life, carry life, birth life, and speak life into a baby as it develops inside of her. However, a woman's ability to bring forth life includes so much more than procreation. It seems God also gave females the nurturing, compassionate, tender, and creative side of His character. Men have these qualities, too, but women can express them more easily than men.

Satan despises anyone or anything that produces life, because it thwarts his evil plan. He is a thief, and his mode of operation is death. The devil hates the spiritual power and influence God has given to His children. He is relentless in his attacks on their potential and on the potential they see in others. He uses a female's sensitivity to taunt her with threats about her, her children, her husband, and those she cherishes. Just as he did in the Garden of Eden, Satan notices when men are not in their appointed position, and women are unprotected, making them easy prey. He'll use whomever and whatever he can to distract her from her brilliant power within. And when he can tempt a male to abandon her physically or emotionally, he thinks of it as a double win for himself and hell. He knows he can destroy an entire generation if he can just get to her heart.

- **Females have a constant radar system.**

God wired women with a sensitive and efficient "radar system." This radar allows a woman to be aware of her environment and provides an internal alarm when necessary, not only for her but also for those she cares about. A woman's radar allows her to think about many things at once and multitask effectively. It also makes it hard for her to focus on just one thing at a time. A woman can stir a pot of chili on the stove, talk on the phone to her friend, greet her husband with a kiss, and think about a meeting at work the next day—all at the same time. A woman's radar also helps her keep track of each family member's whereabouts.

While having an overactive radar is a great strength, it can be exhausting and deplete her energy. It is difficult for a woman to turn off her radar because it's involuntary. Most men think women desire a romantic candlelight dinner because she expects him to deliver something emotionally deep and extravagant. It's more accurate to say that she is longing for a calm and quiet place alone with you so that her radar can slow down. In these settings, she can relax and just be.

Her radar is operating even when she tries to sleep or have a special moment with someone she loves. Just before going to sleep, husbands can invite her to slow down her radar. Reading a book, listening to music, praying, watching a relaxing television show, or engaging in simple, quiet conversation before bed will help.

- **Females are bombarded by the voice of the enemy.**

Most women admit they hear an inner voice of condemnation, competition, comparison, and criticism. Ask a woman about her inadequacies, and she will quickly rattle off a list. Current culture validates her need for perfection.

Christian women know they are made in the image of God, but because of cultural lies, they are hard on themselves. Look around at movies, television, commercials, and social media, and you will see this clearly. What's worse, the enemy turns up the volume as she ages.

MESSAGES A WOMAN HEARS EVERY DAY:

- You're too fat, thin, tall, short, light, or dark.
- She's so much prettier, smarter, and more put together than you are!
- What's wrong with you?
- Buy this, buy that, and you'll feel better about yourself.
- He would have stayed with you (and the kids) if you had been _____.

- You lost that job because you aren't as capable as you thought.

- Act more like a man, and you'll get the next promotion.

It's neverending! Women are so accustomed to this inner voice of criticism, they can hardly shut it off. If you don't believe me, just ask any woman if it's true.

- **Females monitor their environments because environments speak loudly to them.**

It is hard to describe how environments constantly speak to females. Men have told me this surprised them as much as learning about the "female fear factor." To a man, the environment both inside and outside of the home is quiet, but to a woman, the environment is loud.

HOW THE ENVIRONMENT SPEAKS TO A WOMAN:

- The dishes say, "Wash me."

- The bed says, "Make me."

- The clutter says, "Organize me."

- The job says, "What about me?"

- The grocery list says, "Buy me."

- The baby says, "Feed me."

- The text says, "Answer me."

- The clothes say, "Clean and fold me."

- The report card says, "Pay attention to me."

- The aging parent says, "Visit me."

- The friend says, "Have lunch with me."

- The toddler says, "Play with me."

- The lunch boxes say, "Fill me."

- The dinner says, "Prepare me."

- The bills say, "Pay me."

- The car says, "Maintain me."

- The husband says, "Spend time with me."

- The mirror says, "Ugh. Fix me."

- The hair says, "Cut me."

Guys, do you get the idea? Girls, is it true?

Environments both inside and outside of the home are always speaking to women. It is important for them to have some time away from the fray so they can take a bubble bath, read a book, watch a movie, or have lunch with girlfriends. And men, if you need her undivided attention, take her to a place in the house where nothing else is vying for her attention or care.

A special note for husbands: In moments of sexual intimacy, create a quiet atmosphere for her. For a man, sex makes everything right. But for most women, she doesn't feel free to have sex until everything is right. That means the kids are settled and asleep, the dishes are done, and the laundry's put away. You may have heard the old adage, "Sex begins in the kitchen." If men want women to have energy for them, they do well to help her bring her environment into order. A quiet, safe atmosphere will allow her to emotionally connect with you, which can lead to physical connection.

- **Females need time to be creative, arrange, and connect with things in their environment.**

Most men don't witness the creative routines of a woman's life because it usually happens when she is alone. Periodically, a woman will walk through her home or office, moving, relocating, touching, and organizing. It is a way she can connect with what she has collected.

When a woman is alone at home for an extended period, such as when her husband goes out of town, she has more time to focus because she has no one to monitor. Her need to bring forth color and beauty may cause a sudden rush of creativity. Some women may choose to cook, sew, plant, paint, refurbish furniture, or just move through the house straightening a lampshade, pillow, or plant. After a few hours, she may move into the role of protector and provider. She is on high alert without her man on duty. She will make sure all the doors are locked and begin to do things the man in her life usually does. When a man is about to step back into his position of provider and protector after being away, it is helpful if he touches base by texting or calling. A kind, short message might ease the transition for both of them. Unless a rhythm is found and grace is given on both sides, the reentry process may be abrupt and sometimes bumpy. But any transition can be mastered with communication, sensitivity, and authentic care for each other.

I saw this play out during my childhood. When my dad, an airline pilot, was away on a trip, my mom would sew like crazy! She and my dad shared a sewing room/study. So when dad was away on a trip, their shared space became her sewing room. She would rarely come out of the sewing room because her creative time in there alone was limited. As soon as she knew the jet's front tires had hit the runway, she would begin to transition into her usual mode of monitoring my father's well-being.

This is why some women find it challenging when their husbands retire. If the men are always home, the women are always monitoring them. It may seem unnecessary, but she can't stop. It is designed into her female DNA.

- **Females will always find someone or something to love.**

Women are wired for purpose, and her primary purpose is to love. The Bible commands husbands to love their wives, but it urges wives to respect their husbands. Nowhere does it command women to love. Why? I believe it must be because it's more natural for women to love. Females will always find something or someone to pour their love into. Whether they're married, dating, or single, they will discover that much of their purpose is associated with connection. It is beneficial for a woman to be covered by a man who not only understands her need for purpose and love but also helps her achieve it.

The first priority in God's economy is the ministry of the home and the people in it. He designed women to produce beauty, either physically (in her environment) or emotionally (in her people). Godly women create a peaceful atmosphere of love and security for their children and, most importantly, their husbands. How can she do that if she doesn't feel secure? Everyone needs a place of refuge from the storms of life, a place where they feel accepted, nurtured, safe, and loved. The world will beat us up, but women can offer warmth within the walls of the home.

When a man appreciates the fact that a woman is using her God-given gifts for him and those in their family or organization, it causes her to thrive. It is a beautiful thing when a man provides and protects so that a woman can collect, connect, and nurture.

Because of our culture's emphasis upon work, sometimes a woman can feel inferior when she doesn't work outside of the home. Stay-at-home moms have the most important job on the planet, yet they may feel least respected. I used to be shocked when I would go to a business function with Don, and people would ask me what I did.

I would smile and say, "I stay home with our kids and lead Bible studies."

Almost every time, they would quickly snap their heads in the opposite direction and ask the nearest female what *she* did. Their response was dismissive. I don't think they meant to be cruel; they just didn't know what to say next. I have to admit this was discouraging. I had earned a college degree and had built a successful interior design business, but because I chose to stay at home for a time, people acted as though I had less value.

- **Females need emotionally-healthy girlfriends.**

Women need girlfriends. They need a healthy community of friends who are both older and younger. A woman desires to pour and be poured into. She craves friends who fill her up and rarely deplete her. This is a very important part of a woman's world. It is also important for women to understand it's not fair to a man to expect him to do and be what only a girlfriend can. He can never fill that unique role. He can't, no matter how hard he might try.

The essential understanding between girlfriends is that they are designed to connect, communicate, and multiply in a spirit of equity. It becomes a dangerous trap when one woman takes advantage of another woman's inborn desire to nurture. Helping can easily become rescuing and abusive for both. When we start to rescue and enable others, we get in the way of allowing God to teach them to know Him better and trust Him more. God wants us to be sensitive to one another's needs but be careful not to let those needs pull us away from our first ministry, which is our mental and spiritual health, home, and family. It's sad to see the enemy twist the very skills God has given women, and use their God-given design and skills to destroy them. Satan has been watching since the Garden of Eden, and he targeted Eve because he recognized how influential Eve was over Adam.

The enemy's strategy is: *Get the female, and you can take the family.*

This is something I had to learn the hard way. Thinking I was being a "good Christian," I unintentionally let some people suck the life out of me. I thought I was ministering to hurting people, but in many cases, we were both becoming co-dependent. This happens when we take the responsibility for the health and happiness of others. I allowed my own brokenness to drive me to rescue others because I got emotional fulfillment out of it.

Jesus calls us to love people, but sometimes we get confused about what love really is. Enabling someone is not love. Ministry feels energizing at first, but when it is out of balance, even ministry can destroy lives. Far too many well-intentioned Christian women with pure motives can fall into this trap and become addicted to doing "good" and being "needed." It is not healthy. God wants us to ask Him where and when to serve ... and where and when to stop serving. He wants us to identify His voice, hear His directives, and confidently obey.

When all is said and done, females have a distinguished role in the Kingdom of God. Whether or not they are married, women represent the passionate desire of our Savior. What do I mean?

Well, God could have chosen any metaphor to explain His church, but He didn't describe it as a tribe or an army.

He described the church as His Bride.

This choice of words has exquisite implications. No one can ever say that the Lord does not value women. In fact, right now, the church is on His heart.

And one day, Jesus will return for ... *her*.

KEY #3 FOR WOMEN: COMMUNICATE

How can males communicate with the females
in their lives to gain trust?

In our current culture, there are too many jokes about female communication to count. The stereotypes include: Women talk too much, and men "can't get a word in edgewise." Women nag, nag, nag. Women let people know they are upset by scolding them or giving them the silent treatment. Women are emotionally unpredictable. Women are grouchy and rude during "that time of the month."

This negative list could go on and on while the true beauty of communicating with a woman is largely disregarded. The concepts listed in this chapter will help women understand and appreciate themselves, and other women. Most importantly, they will turn on a light of revelation for men who have longed to solve the mystery of communication with a woman.

- **Females need to feel nurtured and cherished by the males in their lives.**

A woman feels most cherished and nurtured when she is free to be her feminine self. She longs to have a trustworthy man who is available to hold her emotionally and physically. Imagine a man using one arm to hold a woman close to him, while using his other arm to hold a sword to protect her. Regardless of the continent or culture, every woman is designed to desire this figurative scenario. A man's strength should not be used to threaten or overpower a woman but to care for, provide for, and cover her. A woman who is not covered by a man may close her heart to him, isolate herself, and become withdrawn around him. This can bring a sense of *oppression*, which can lead to *depression*. The deeper she slides into the hole, the more work and time will be required to coax her out.

I've had the privilege of taking this message to Tokyo, Japan, and I wondered if the keys would translate across cultural lines. After I shared the message, it was clear these concepts truly are universal. A wife needs a husband to cover her by showing gentleness and understanding, even when she is undeserving. Isn't that Christ's heart, even when His Bride, the church, disappoints Him? When a man is in the Word and listening to the Lord, the words he speaks over his wife bring power and life.

The Message depicts Ephesians 5:25–28 so beautifully:

"Husbands, go all out in your love for your wives, exactly as Christ did for the church—a love marked by giving, not getting. Christ's love makes the church whole. His words evoke her beauty. Everything he does and says is designed to bring the best out of her, dressing her in dazzling white silk, radiant with holiness. And that is how husbands ought to love their wives. They're really doing themselves a favor—since they're already 'one' in marriage."

It is as if God gave married men the gift of their bride, and they have the awesome privilege of caring for her well and presenting her soul and spirit back to the Father in heaven in beautiful condition.

- **Females respond well to emotional intimacy.**

A woman needs to know that the significant men in her life want to connect with her emotionally. Females need males who will listen and partner with them. Ask her about her thoughts concerning decisions, and share your thoughts with her. Nothing is a substitute for connecting emotionally through conversation. Flowers, gifts, dinners, and get-away trips can be fun but can trigger disappointment later if there is no emotional connection. It is not wise to use trips as a distraction or as a bandage. Women appreciate gifts that say, "I thought of you," not only because it is a holiday or because the giver needs her forgiveness.

One Thanksgiving not too long ago, our children were spending the holiday with their in-laws so Don and I decided to go on a trip, just the two of us. Don really wanted to go on a cruise, but I was nervous. We hadn't been on a trip alone (with no business associates, friends, family, or kids) since our honeymoon. On a cruise, there would be no Internet. No work to do.

No friends. No distractions. Just us. I was afraid that our emotional healing might not be as deep as I'd hoped. What if Don disconnected like he had for years? What if we slid back into familiar patterns? Now that our kids were grown, married, and settled into their individual lives, would we still have things to talk about? Would he still be able to be gentle with me, or would he hurt my feelings?

We'd come so far, and I was afraid of a setback. Thankfully, we had a wonderful time and found that we were more connected than ever. Because of the keys, we've learned to appreciate our differences and give each other grace. We no longer take things personally, and we enjoy being partners and friends. Our time alone on the cruise made us want to do it again, and soon!

- **Females need verbal approval.**

Women are designed to notice and respond to the moods of people in their lives, especially males. A man's mood immediately changes her environment. If her husband, boyfriend, father, or brother seems to be bothered, discontent, or in a bad mood, she will try (even subconsciously) to find out what's wrong and make it better. God designed her as his helper. Because it's important for her to have order in her environment, she will do what she can to bring peace to her home or workplace. When men are not happy, she will automatically assume it's because of something she did. So when she asks how she can help, and men don't say anything, it perpetuates her mistaken assumption.

Does this mean that a man can never be in a bad mood? Of course not. It's just helpful if he communicates about it. If a woman thinks the men in her world are not pleased, her safety and security are rocked, and she begins to move from one thing to the next, trying different approaches to improve his attitude or mood. What she is saying is, "Do you see me? Can you hear me? Am I important to you? Are you pleased with me? Are you still going to protect me?"

Men should let a woman know when his bad mood is not her fault. And if his unhappy demeanor *is* connected to something she did, he should share that with her in a considerate way. She wants him to be pleased with her and to enjoy his role as provider and protector. When men do not handle moods this way and ignore a woman's attempt to please or keep him, she may become more needy and less secure.

It can be damaging when men take their natural strength for granted and raise their voices. Even if she knows his mood is not her fault, it can shatter a woman's heart when a man speaks loudly and harshly. Men can act like a drill sergeant or football coach with one another, but it doesn't work when communicating with a woman. She will disconnect, remove herself from the situation, or become "masculinized." She'll self-protect in every way she knows how. If a man pays attention, he will see the disappointment on a woman's face when he raises his voice. Remember, females are transparent like a beautiful lead crystal pitcher and not that difficult to read if you watch.

A woman is highly sensitive to the criticism of men, particularly if they don't ever encourage her. If a man genuinely expresses his verbal approval from time to time, the females in his life will eagerly listen, feel heard, supported, and valued by him. Women who are fortified with encouraging words are more confident and, in turn, are more honoring and supportive of men.

A woman thrives when she hears sincere compliments about her physical appearance.

Husbands, your wife needs to know she is the most beautiful girl in the world to you. She needs to hear it from the most important men in her world. If a woman doesn't feel valuable to the most important men in her world, it can drive her toward another man she feels she can please. Satan is more than happy to give her options.

In the early years of our marriage (before I became a Christian), I stepped dangerously close to the edge of this pit. Because neither Don nor I knew any of these keys, he would get busy with work and become distracted and would emotionally shut off from me. I couldn't get him to "see me." Before we had our kids, I was working full-time, running my design business, where I often interacted with wealthy, attractive men. While I didn't have a physical affair with another man, my mind was completely involved in an emotional affair. Satan had his laser pointed at the wound in my heart, and my loneliness made me susceptible. The enemy tried to convince me that another man could offer me everything my husband couldn't at the time.

Thankfully, Jesus was laser-focused on my situation, too. He came and gave me a way out. I look back at that time and realize I was walking too close to a fire; it's a miracle I didn't get burned. The Lord protected me from myself. I am often reminded of what my rebellion could have cost me. I would never have known two of the greatest gifts of my life, Jonathan and Holly. I would have missed knowing their spouses and our priceless four grandchildren.

- **Females overtalk when they feel insecure or disconnected.**

When a woman feels nervous, devalued, unprotected, or exposed, she can have a tendency to "overtalk." Women are designed to bring connection, and connection comes through talking.

Insecurity in a woman causes her to talk, out of a fear of rejection. It can be a defense mechanism. When I was wounded and insecure, I overtalked (which still happens if I don't stay alert). Don used to make fun of me because he did not understand why I was like this. He used to be very quiet and introverted. When we were with friends, and I started feeling insecure about myself and embarrassed about "Don's silence," I would talk out of nervousness to fill the space.

Sometimes Don would make a sarcastic comment like, "She breathes through her ears."

It was hurtful, and I overcompensated by talking even more. Now that he knows why I overtalk, he doesn't think it's funny because he recognizes it as a signal that I am feeling unsafe. This key has been a tremendous help to us.

Men, if a woman in your life is overly talkative, you might want to ask the Lord why she's overtalking. She may feel exposed, unprotected, and insecure, and in some cases you may be the person she is protecting herself from. Make an effort to emotionally cover and validate her, then see what happens.

- **Females withhold physically, verbally, and emotionally when they feel devalued or used.**

Most women only share emotionally with people they trust. When a woman ceases to communicate (with men or women), it may mean she doesn't trust the person or has, for some reason, felt a need to disconnect from them.

Picture a man or woman asking a female, "How was your day?" She might answer, "Fine."

Then they might ask, "Were you busy at work, or was it slow?"

If she responds with another short answer, such as, "It was normal," that's a good sign there is something wrong. A female almost always takes time to give details, because she is wired to connect with people. Warm, connected conversation usually includes details and descriptions (of good and bad situations) about her day at work. It's a sign of relational health when men invite women to share, and they share and share and share and share. It means she feels safe.

If someone asked a man what he did on Saturday, he would probably answer something like, "I went to Home Depot." But if someone asked a female the same question, she would give them a "collection report." She might list each errand she ran, who she saw, what they talked about, and how it made her feel. She has been collecting pieces of information all day. It's in her nature to polish the pieces she has collected to try to make something beautiful out of them.

Collectors sometimes take visual pictures to remember the area so they can revisit the good experiences again.

Men are the opposite. They may take notes of places to hide and wait because they are hunting or positioning themselves for success. So even if you don't understand or care about what the women in your life are sharing, you could choose connection and love them enough to let them pour. The longer you let her pour, the more room she will have for you.

When a man doesn't listen to a woman, she notices. Over time, if she can't get him to connect with her, she may begin to lose her "voice." She'll stop believing that her words have value. When women lose their voice, something inside of them dies. Because women are wired to connect, communication is very important to their mental and emotional health. If she believes she has lost her voice, she is in danger of giving up her God-given influence and power. Not being able to use her voice to speak life, give input, or make an impact causes a female to slowly decay from the inside out. Men, this is an intensely scary place for a female of any age to be.

Males are not wired with or for the same purpose as a woman, and this may be a hard concept for them to understand.

Satan enjoys kicking women while they're down, because he is ruthless and relentless.

His goal is to shatter her and everyone connected to her. Satan has been observing males and females from the beginning, and he knows women want to please the men who are supposed to provide for and protect them. He also knows women can hide pain, rejection, and disappointment out of the fear that they will be displeasing to men. Satan strategizes so that something will trigger the pain she has tried to ignore. That is when a complete "shatter" occurs.

First, a woman loses her voice, either temporarily or long-term. Then she loses her sense of self. Next, she may suddenly shock everyone by exploding into one million pieces. She will scream or cry uncontrollably. These outbursts can surprise her, too.

Men, a "shatter" is more than a crack or break. It resembles dynamite in a piece of crystal. Pain of this magnitude will probably only occur if you are unaware of cracks that happen repeatedly. I have only experienced this three times in more than 40 years.

But here is the good news. You have been given the ability to put her back together again.

This takes focus, time, and patience on your part. It is worth it if you deeply care about her.

- **Females of all ages can be calmed or emotionally anchored by non-sexual touch.**

Touch is a powerful way to offer peace to a woman. When a trustworthy male touches a woman in a non-sexual way by holding her hand, touching her shoulder or knee, or putting his hand on the small of her back, it centers and calms her immediately. It lets her know he is there for her, focused on her, and ready to take care of and protect her. Whether driving down the road, walking through the kitchen, strolling through a shopping area, or reaching across the table at dinner to hold her hand, a woman feels emotionally anchored when a man touches her. Even an intentional look from across a room lets a woman know that he is available, aware, and that she is important to him.

Be aware that a touch is not a substitute for emotional and verbal connection. When a touch is used in place of verbal and emotional intimacy, one of two things may happen: 1) She may question the authenticity of the man. 2) She may disconnect emotionally, spiritually, and intellectually because she feels manipulated. Taking time to talk to her in a meaningful way will increase your connection and build trust in her.

The power of a male's touch extends beyond marriage. Please lean in and pay attention, here. There is an appropriate way for men to touch women who are not their wives. Yet, in a day and age when men are leary of accusation and misunderstanding, we have almost eliminated wholesome touch between a man and a woman. We all know that touch can be motivated by foul intentions, but not every male-to-female touch is bad. Platonic touch can be described as courteous, chivalrous, polite, thoughtful, and gentlemanly. The perfect example of a polite touch is "the helping hand." When a man offers a helping hand to a woman by opening a door for her, helping her out of a car, or negotiating a tight space, she feels safe. Men, you are equipped to offer help and protection to any woman, not just the ones you know well. Some women may have rejected your offers, but that is her issue. God sees your heart and motive. And remember, women were designed to feel valued and cared for when you do. Some women remember the kindness of a touch for decades.

Recently, a 79 year-old woman shared a memory of a polite touch from a male stranger.

She was 12 and was enjoying the day with her friends at an amusement park. A kind man noticed that she was being jostled by the crowd in line for a popular ride. He put out one hand to halt the overeager people and one hand on her back to guide her through the turnstile. By the time she spun around to thank him, he was already absorbed by the crowd. She smiled warmly as she remembered a brief moment of protective touch that happened more than sixty years ago.

- **Females assume men are angry when they are quiet.**

A female often assumes when a man doesn't share details, he is intentionally withholding information from her. She may even go so far as to believe he is punishing her. Why? Because "the silent treatment" is one way women communicate extreme displeasure with someone, even though she may know it is an unhealthy habit. So a woman believes whatever is going on to cause his silence is her fault, and she tries to fix it. The truth is, in most cases, men don't talk simply because they don't have anything to say. Letting a woman know you just want to be quiet and that it's not personal is a gift to her.

Here are two more helpful reminders for males about communicating with females:

First, when you communicate with men, you may want to omit details that he might not find necessary. On the other hand, when you are sharing with females, the most basic information is not always sufficient from a woman's point of view. She may want more details, not because she is snooping or trying to control you but because she deeply desires connection with you.

Secondly, if a woman asks you to go get something for her at the grocery store, she will probably try to give you lots of specific details. She may even tell you the exact aisle and shelf, as well as the color and design of the box. It's important to remember she does this because she is trying to make it easier for you. She forgets you like to hunt for things. It can be hurtful and destructive if you interrupt and cut her off. She is wired to give details and help, but if you shut her down by saying, "Okay, okay! I've got it!" what she hears is, "I don't need you."

It may sound strange, but most women feel this way at their core, whether they can articulate it or not. Her biggest fear is being discounted, rejected, or unprotected. To her, if you don't think what she says is important, she starts to feel like you may not value her enough to protect her, and that can feel earth-shattering to her. This is one of the reasons women may blow things out of proportion. The smallest turning away from her can become a deep wound in her heart. That's because women are designed to multiply everything: the good *and* the bad.

- **Females who receive unexplained "no's" feel controlled and disconnected and will eventually respond by emasculating the male who is saying no.**

Women may offer help to men, but when one who has a higher income or perceived power over her passes out an unexplained "no," she will feel controlled. If a husband or male superior often denies her requests, a woman will respect his decision, but only if he takes the time to explain his reasoning. If a denial comes without a reason why, a female may usurp a male's authority and emasculate him as a defense mechanism because she is hurt, angry, frustrated, or frightened. The "no" feels like it is being sent down from a judge and jury.

Men, whether it's spending money or making decisions for an organization or a family, explaining a "no" can build unity and bring validation. Remember, regardless of income or power, if you are in a relationship, you are equal partners on the same team.

- **Female emotions reside deep within their hearts and eventually emerge in ways that are evident in their entire body.**

When a female feels deep emotion, it will usually come out of her entire body and include a word or a noise. Whether it is joy, sadness, anxiety, or fear, she will often show emotion all over her face. When the feeling is extreme, she will almost always move her body and make a noise. Her emotions come from a deep place in her heart that they resonate through her entire being.

She may squeal or cry. Some women bend at the waist and put their hands over their mouths or up in the air. Some jump for joy or kneel on the ground, as if the emotion that began deep within has finally made its way out. The next time you go to a play or a movie and something deeply emotional happens in the storyline, listen carefully for the sounds that come out of the audience. More than likely, they're coming from women.

Female emotions lie just beneath the surface, and when they emerge, they can be surprising to males.

- **Females feel crushed when the males in their lives look at or lust after other females.**

It breaks a woman's heart when a man looks at or lusts after another woman. It makes her feel inadequate and unimportant. Regardless of what she may or may not say, it destroys her trust in him and wounds her to the core. It is not only destructive to their relationship, it sets a horrible example for their children.

To his daughter it says, "Men need more, and are never satisfied." To his son it says, "This is what men do."

Men have a small window of opportunity to establish and model the value of women to any who may be watching. It's sad when children pick up bad behaviors from their home environment and develop core lies that can start a cascade of pain for generations.

Years ago the Lord spoke to my heart and said, "Be sure you are raising your children in a way you will enjoy watching when they are parents because more than likely, you will see it all again."

What a sobering thought. God takes relationships and parenting very seriously, and we are wise to do so, too.

My hope is that the keys for women have been eye-opening for men and women alike. The Bible describes women as physically weaker than men. However, only females can emotionally and physically conceive, carry, and give birth to the entire world's population.

First Peter 3:7 says, "Husbands, in the same way be considerate as you live with your wives, and treat them with respect as the weaker partner and as heirs with you of the gracious gift of life, so that nothing will hinder your prayers" (NIV). Males and females are simply different. Does this mean that the female body might be more vulnerable or fragile than a male's, regardless of how hard she may try to build muscle mass and bone density? Whether we like it or not, ladies, I believe it does.

Women of all ages are drawn to men who demonstrate steady strength, calm, support, and security. God created women to need the safe, masculine, strength that only a good man can offer. Females thrive in this environment when it is available.

TESTIMONIALS FROM WOMEN

I entered my second marriage, coming from a very toxic, abusive marriage, carrying lots of baggage that I "dumped" on my kind, loving new husband. I had always had to carry all the responsibility alone: finances, the home, the children. It was hard to let go and trust someone. I had so much fear that they were going to disappoint me or let me fall. Cristie's keys were pivotal in our marriage. The one that speaks volumes to me is men's desire to protect and provide, and women's need to feel secure and valued. After we understood these natural roles that God had created for our relationship, we were able to talk more openly about our needs in a safe and secure space where we both felt respected, valued, and heard.

Renee R.

The keys completely blew me away—in the best way! It's helped me love and lead better, not just in my personal relationships, but also with the amazing team I get to do life and ministry with. These truths unlocked so much healing, honor, and understanding that now I can't not see the beauty in how God designed both men and women!

Amy Ford Founder Embrace Grace, Inc.

The keys have been a part of our family's story since the beginning. They have been woven into the tapestry of my husband's and my marriage. From the understanding of needing to allow men to "unwind" at the end of the day (when I really want to pour all of my words into him at once) to the realization that I'm not crazy, God created me to have a constant radar system, Cristie's words consistently surface in our everyday thinking. We read the book while engaged and continue to apply the message. I firmly believe the keys have helped me to not only understand my husband more fully, but they've helped me to understand myself. And now I fully appreciate the gender roles God designated for our two sons and our daughter. This is a book that our family will turn to over and over again, for many years to come. And surely will fall into the hands of our three children as they mature in age. We are grateful for every single page.

Claire A.

We were standing around the kitchen as Cristie shared these beautiful keys to a group of women who were either engaged or newly married. It was such a different perspective from what we had been taught by society, and we were all changed. She relayed practical ways to grow as a couple and to be effective parents, and friends. Her insights still help me after that kitchen conversation 12 years ago. The book that followed reinforced and further showed me as a wife, mother, and grandmother how to encourage in a way that builds the everlasting beauty of God's design for His children. I can't recommend this material enough.

Kathy A.

The female truths have resonated deeply in me. I found my guard dropping as I realized why I feel the way I do-it's innate, okay, and even good! God has wired me uniquely female and has purposes and plans in that. Some of the standouts for me were female radar systems, fear factor, and contentment monitoring. The male truths are both eye-opening and constructive. After studying my own husband and other males in my life for many years, this book has revealed several blind spots for me to learn and grow. The male truths both affirm me and challenge me to be a better wife, mom, and female in general. Transition time, bullet points, and the need for men to try and learn new things are some of the first truths to help me grow in understanding.

Leanne B.

I highly recommend studying the keys. With every reread, I continue to find treasured information that seems to hit me harder and harder. Society tells us, as well as our kids, one thing, and we need books like this to bring us back to the basics of who God designed us to be. I will continue to reference what I've learned as I get older and form new relationships with females, as well as navigate the relationships I now have with both males and females.

Holli M.

IN NEED OF RESCUE

The very day I call for help, the tide of battle turns. My enemies flee! This one thing I know: God is for me! I am trusting God—oh, praise his promises! I am not afraid of anything mere man can do to me! Yes, praise his promises.

Psalm 56:9-11 TLB

Satan's intentional targeting of unprotected females became vividly clear to me when Don and I traveled to Greece on a mission trip supporting Christine Caine's ministry, The A21 Campaign. A21 is a non-profit, non-governmental organization that rescues girls trafficked for the sex trade and works to bring traffickers to justice.

Before we arrived, our team leaders warned us to be spiritually prepared and prayed up—we were about to encounter the raw aftermath of human trafficking. Still, nothing could have truly prepared us for what we would witness.

The stories we heard were gut-wrenching. The underground network of trafficking felt more like something out of a horror movie than reality. It was shocking, and at times, almost impossible to believe. Then we looked into their eyes—these young women were now free but still bearing the deep scars of their past. Their innocence had been stolen. Yet behind their pain, we also saw deep gratitude. Gratitude for freedom. Gratitude for hope.

This experience changed us to our core. It wasn't just about helping them—it was also about us being transformed. In those moments, a holy determination was born in us: to educate others, to expose darkness, and to stand for truth.

The women told stories of how family members sent them to find work so they could send money back home. Instead, they were trapped in a brothel, without access to their passports, and they were brutally forced to "service" many men each day. They wanted freedom so badly they risked their lives to escape captivity. Their courage was staggering. Thankfully, they were now in a safe place, going to school or learning a trade, and hearing about the God who wants to take care of them and heal their hearts.

As we listened to their stories, we were surprised to hear so many different accents. The fact that they originated from so many different countries was a stark reminder that Satan's plan to destroy women is global. Sex trafficking not only assaults the victim, but the God who made them.

Satan has been observing humans since the beginning of mankind, and he knows the damage we can do to the kingdom of darkness when we yield to God's authority and accept our true identities. Even if we have not experienced the horror of human trafficking, after reading through the keys for both men and women, you may have realized that you have been enslaved by a misunderstanding of the opposite gender for a long time. Perhaps you feel as if the enemy has stolen your gender identity—your "passport" to access blessed relationships here on earth. As a result, you may be living in a dark situation at work, at home, in your marriage, or with certain friends.

Take heart. Yes, Satan is constantly on the prowl, looking for someone to devour. But Jesus is always on a mission, looking for someone to rescue. If God allows an attack, He has plans to use it for our good and possibly the good of others. Through every battle or struggle, He promises to grow us, mature us, and display His glory through us. Nothing is over until He says it's over, and He wants to use everything—yes, *everything*. He allows circumstances for His glory and ultimate purpose on earth, even if we can't fully understand.

God reveals so He can heal. God rescues so He can restore. Even so, at the point of rescue, the process of restoration has just begun. Just like it was for the human trafficking victims we met in Greece, a person can be set free but still need time to heal. Remember that this kind of healing requires commitment, time, perseverance, and cooperation with God. Please don't expect your relationships to snap into place and operate in a healthy way overnight, simply because your eyes have been opened by these keys. When someone has completely shut down in a relationship, it may take days, months, or even years for them to "come back to life." Even in platonic relationships, hearts are most vulnerable at the point of rescue, and your friend or co-worker may be hesitant to trust you. Respecting their space and staying committed by showing genuine, consistent transformation through your words and behavior will begin to build a bridge if both parties desire it.

This is especially important within marriage. These wounds can be deeper because the love, covenant, and connections are much more intense. In some cases, a deep relational fracture can be complicated by infidelity. If an extra-marital affair has occurred, then intense prayer, intentional effort, and professional counseling may be critical to the restoration process. In every meaningful interaction, ask the Lord what He wants to say to your spouse and yield to His directive, instead of your own desires. Power and healing are in His words, which are always more adequate than your own.

There is no substitute for submitting to God's guidance in our relationships, and it is never more critical than at the beginning. It may feel awkward to start living from a new perspective. Every now and then, you might even find yourself falling back into old habits, even after your relationships have been healed. For instance, when I finally decided to obey the Lord and write this book, Don and I planned time for me to take a couple of trips alone to our lake house so I could write without interruption. About three weeks before I was scheduled to leave, he seemed distracted and disconnected, which triggered fear in me. He was home physically, but not emotionally. As the distance between us continued to grow, Don began exhibiting some old behaviors I hadn't seen in a while. It would have been easy for me to ignore it and just let him "drift" while I gave him grace. I pretended I was being sacrificial, but I was really protecting myself from disappointment. I had done that for years, but after the keys, I knew it was not productive. And, frankly, it was self-serving.

"Lord," I prayed, "I don't know why this is happening, but I don't want to be disappointed or feel rejected again. Please help us get out of this familiar downward spiral!"

Any time we are about to launch out in obedience and do something the Lord is asking us to do, the enemy studies our behavior and sets traps that have worked against us in the past.

Satan knew I was preparing to share with the world something the Lord had downloaded into my heart. He knew the keys were a message that could potentially save marriages, restore people, and heal families. He would do anything to keep these keys from being brought to life.

I continued to pray as the date for my writing retreat approached. Meanwhile, I became more and more worried as Don "blew by me on the fast track," seemingly in another world. I made excuses for him, telling myself that his emotional distance had nothing to do with me, and that I should be thankful he was providing for me. However, that was part of the old pattern and part of the trap.

Eventually, I pulled away into silence and self-protection. Then, we were both back in the trap. I have to admit if I had taken the time to sit down and gently and respectfully ask Don what was going on, things might have stopped there. But weeks passed, and just two days before I was to leave for the lake, I snapped. I mean, I *really* snapped.

What did it look like?

I insulted him. In a flash, I verbally pulled out my "sword" and slashed at Don, emasculating him in front of our adult kids. It was not nearly as brutal as it used to be, and the kids did not recognize it as harsh, but Don did. I could tell by the look on his face.

Realizing what I'd done, I waited until we were alone to apologize and ask for his forgiveness. Don did the same. In a tender conversation where we finally reconnected, Don said he was shocked that we had gone "there" again. We had been adversaries for years, and we were accustomed to the pain. But now that we are partners who really care for and try to understand one another, the consequences of our old habits were excruciating. We had further to fall than we used to, and it deeply hurt both of our hearts to mistreat one another. We both shed tears that night because we were so disappointed to have "done it again."

But Don and I were able to get back on track quickly. We were determined to be more cautious and aware than ever. He gave me permission to signal him at the first sign of slipping, and I did the same.

Then Don encouraged me, even more strongly, to go to the lakehouse and write this book. "I believe the Lord allowed us to fall into that 'trap' so you could write about it. You have to warn people there will be traps, which often trigger others. Once we are both in the cycle, it requires attention, desire, and effort from both to stop and reverse it. They will fall, but they can press into the Lord and into one another to get to the other side. Tell people not to quit; the benefits are worth it!"

Take Don's word for it: this is worth the work. We know we will trip up again, and you will, too. But the Lord will always be there to pick us up, dust us off, dry our tears, and set us back on our feet.

Have you ever sensed God calling you to pursue something impossible? I want to acknowledge that you may be feeling that way today. You have glimpsed the hope of heaven for your relationships with the opposite gender, but restoration may seem too far away. Maybe even finding out that Don and I can still slip back into old habits scares you.

I have felt that way; we are all human. When you are at the point of rescue, and your eyes have been opened, it can be a shock. My best advice is to move forward a little bit at a time. I was in prayer one day when the Lord showed me a clear visual of what that looks like.

I saw myself standing on one side of an altar. The Father was on the other. It felt like I had been ushered into a holy place.

God stood behind a thick marble slab between us. He had a kind but intense demeanor. Then He placed something resembling a large pie on the altar. It looked dark, chunky, and thick. It smelled bad, and it was not easy to look at. I wondered why something so disgusting would be allowed here.

The Lord took a large, sharp knife and began to cut a piece out of the nasty pie. He placed it on a plate, and, looking into my eyes,

He slid it toward me. My eyes began to fill with tears as I saw the sadness on His face.

Then he asked me a question. "Cristie, I understand that this is hard, and you feel alone with the weight of these keys. The battle is fierce, but are you willing to take one piece of My pain?" Immediately, I felt overwhelming conviction. God has been deeply hurt by the corruption of His divine design for males and females. Yet there was something I could do. By taking a small piece of His pain, I could feel the ache of this confused generation. Would I choose to work on my relationships and help other people work on theirs? Or would I walk away and leave it all with Him because it's too painful?

He continued, "I am giving it to you. I provided the heavy burden and followed it with enough passion for you to carry it out. I knew you would take both. I built you as a truth teller and a trailblazer. I have given this to you as a gift. I wanted you to experience what I feel regarding my Bride, the Church. I understand it is painful for you, but I promise it will be worth it in the end. There will be a reward. You will experience My glory over this issue, whether you see it on earth or someday in heaven. Watching my Bride suffer extreme pain and disappointment in a continual downward spiral is more painful to Me than you can imagine. I want you to share a portion, but I will take it back if you don't want it."

We get to choose day by day and moment by moment, and I believe He is saying the same thing to you. Will you take a small piece of His pain and accept the burden to change, no matter how long it takes and no matter how much it costs?

One of my favorite prayers is: *Lord, help me to believe that You are who You say You are, and help me believe that I am who You say I am!*

We can never become who God has called us to be until we understand what His Word says and activate it through faith and His powerful Holy Spirit.

I know you wish that you could just get it right, *right now*. But we humans have a lot more habits to break and a lot more lessons to learn before we find ourselves at the wedding feast of the Lamb, where we get to take our seats as the Bride of Christ. On that beautiful day, Jesus, the Bridegroom of heaven, will be our gracious host. He is even more eager for that day than we are.

IN POSITION FOR RESET

The old life is gone; a new life emerges! Look at it!
All this comes from the God who settled the relationship
between us and him, and then called us to settle
our relationships with each other.

2 Corinthians 5:17 MSG

"My husband left me with five children," one woman shared when she approached me after my presentation about the keys. "He was emotionally incapable of being a provider and protector. If I had known about these keys when we were dating, I would have known my identity as a woman, and I would have seen he was not emotionally healthy enough to walk in his as a man. I really wish I had understood all of this back then."

This sweet woman taught me something of great value. As we courageously position ourselves by faith, it is wise to watch what the opposite gender does. Stepping into the fullness of your role may cause some confusion and challenges in healthy relationships, and it might end a few unhealthy ones. The restoration of our identity takes time. Ask God to give you the discernment and wisdom to act on what He is putting before you. God can heal anyone who is willing to be teachable, but when we're not, He will not force us. Don't try to force anyone into a new way of thinking. Let God soften their hearts. Remember that it only takes one person to begin the repositioning of a couple, family, workplace, organization, or culture. As we partner with God and are led by His Spirit, He will help us all the way through. We don't have to get stuck. Resist the urge to lean away from uncomfortable situations because the old way seems easier. Be bold and brave—you are not alone, you are partnering with the Creator of the Universe. Repositioning takes commitment, requires purposefulness, and is a process. Just as it takes a while to build physical muscle memory in order to change lifestyle habits, it takes a while to build spiritual muscle memory in order to change emotional habits. Remember, we have the amazing power of the Holy Spirit to help us.

Why does He care so much about the way males and females interact with each other?

Because when men and women don't step into the identity God has for us, His plans are aborted. That is also true of the divine relationship Jesus has with His Bride (the Church). He longs for her to take her "feminine" role and receive His "masculine" provision and protection. Did you notice? God wired women to need exactly what the Bride of Christ needs. The church was created to reflect beauty, to collect and connect people, to transform environments for the better, and to pour Living Water over the globe, bringing forth life. Women are like that. The church can abort God's plans or give birth to them. There is no end to what females will accomplish for the Kingdom if they position themselves according to their divine design. When she operates in her power and strength by submitting to the wisdom and authority of her Bridegroom, Jesus, the entire earth is affected.

When I think of God's plans being aborted, I can't help but think of the profound influence of one lost female by the name of Madalyn Murray O'Hair. She founded American Atheists and challenged mandatory Bible reading and prayer in public schools in *Murray v. Curlett*, a case that went all the way to the Supreme Court in 1963.

As we all know, she won. And the United States legalized abortion just ten years later. That is more than just a coincidence; it is a spiritual attack on family, women, and the One who designed them.

O'Hair famously said, "An atheist believes that a hospital should be built instead of a church. An atheist believes that deed must be done instead of prayer said. An atheist strives for involvement in life and not escape into death. He wants disease conquered, poverty vanished, war eliminated."

Sadly, this quote almost seems reasonable to many people today because of the indoctrination of mainstream media. That is how much we have changed since Bible reading and prayer ceased being a foundational component of education.

We could lament this national loss without hope, or we could take up the challenge set by O'Hair's evil example. If one bold woman, under the power of Satan, can start such a damaging cultural movement, what would we do as the women of God with the power of the Holy Spirit? What do you think? Does that inspire you? We can change the tide of history if the church gets educated and walks in her identity by honoring God and His original design for males and females.

Spiritually speaking, the church should not be trying to do what only God can do, and God will not do what the church should be doing.

Why did it take so long for me to receive the keys that would not only change my marriage, but save my life? I spent a lot of time asking God why it took so long, and He showed me that when there is lack, He wants to provide purpose. He can always use our pain if we want to learn. No matter how long you have struggled, He can show you how to take your position and be the man or woman He made you to be.

I pray He won't have to prove it to you as dramatically as He did for me.

The experience that finally helped me "get it" began when our church's women's ministry department asked me to be in a promotional video to advertise the annual women's conference. The request was humbling and, honestly, scary. This church has international exposure and influence. Not only would their sanctuary be filled with thousands of guests, the conference would include hundreds of watch parties all over the globe.

Though I didn't know any details of the video shoot, I knew I was supposed to say "yes." Weeks went by. Then I got the call that they had dropped off the dress that I would be wearing for the video, and the package was on my front porch.

I felt panic well up in my heart. What had I agreed to? Suddenly, I felt self-conscious about being 67 years old, 5'2," and twenty pounds heavier than I'd ever been. I was short, thick, and felt old. I felt sure I was the female representative for the older generation in our church.

I heard the Lord whisper, "You can do this."

I got the dress off our porch and held my breath while unwrapping it in the privacy of my closet. With an anxious heart, I pulled out a blush-colored, sparkling, Queen-like dress.

As I stood in the closet and looked at myself in the full-length mirror, I sighed. The dress was okay, but I did not like it on me. I had struggled with my weight all my life and had been verbally criticized by my dad continuously. My only sister was 5'8" and beautiful. She'd had the stature of a queen, and as I looked at myself in that ball gown, I felt like the little girl who was pretending. I began to wish I had not agreed to participate in the video shoot.

"Will you trust Me?" the Lord asked.

I looked in the mirror and fought back tears. Then I took off the dress and left the closet.

The day of the outdoor video shoot arrived. I put on the dress one more time. After hair and makeup, we drove to the location for filming. Everyone unloaded and began the steep climb up the rocky hill. With a glance, I saw it. There was a huge white enamel throne sitting atop the 90-foot cliff, with the east sun rising behind it. The air was still, and no one spoke for a while.

Women of different ages were playing a role in the event, and we were all dressed like queens. We looked at each other in wonder. Then a member of the ministry team placed a crown on my head, and said with an endearing smile, "You are beautiful, Cristie. Do you feel beautiful?" I knew that was her heart's desire for me, and I did not want to lie, so I said, "It is humbling and hard to receive."

Once again, the Lord whispered into my heart, "That is how they see you, Cristie. This is an honor; you need to believe it and receive it." He continued, "Can you stop focusing on yourself? Can you let Me use you at this age—just as you are—to bless and speak to My girls your age?"

Following their directions (and the Lord's), I approached the massive throne, turning slowly and as gracefully as I could on the rocky cliff. Then I sat down without a word, trying to muster the regal authority of a queen.

I did it, but it was uncomfortable. I had to keep repeating in my mind, "Cristie, this is not about *you*."

Next, the kind young director asked me to stand on the cliff and glance over the water as if it were my kingdom. I knew the Lord was standing right there with me. Ironically, I was looking over the exact spot on the same lake where we had raised our kids at our family lakehouse!

Finally, the shoot was over. Afterward, one of the photographers asked me to go to his laptop to see the images. He was enthusiastic as we all gathered around the screen, saying, "Look at you! You are beautiful! Don't you love these photos?"

When I looked at the images, I gasped. No one knew that the gasp was because in the photographs of me, all I saw was my grandmother. It wasn't a bad thing, but I have to say it was shocking.

Three days later, I was driving to a friend's house when the Lord's sweet but authoritative voice spoke to my heart. "Cristie, I am proud of you. Thank you for what you did, but I must ask, when will you emotionally and spiritually take your position?"

I thought to myself, *I did what you asked me to do, Lord. What else could you want of me?*

Because God can hear our thoughts, He replied, "In your mind, you have repeatedly relived the moment of walking up to that throne and taking your seat. Now, please do it emotionally and spiritually! You are not in your thirties so expecting to look like it or act like it is offensive to Me. Do not be ashamed of your age or your body. I made you, and not accepting yourself is an insult to Me. You are who you are; you have lived through trauma and pain, and you have grown and found freedom from it. Take your life experiences and step into your spiritual position! Be the mature queen I have equipped you to be. Please don't waste your pain or My work in you. Culture has fed you and your beautiful sisters a lie about age and physical beauty. I chose you for the video shoot because I am proud of your growth. I love you, and I have plans for you! Will you let Me use you? If so, let's get to it."

I finally took my position that day in my car, and I have never been the same.

Are you wondering whatever happened to that promotional video? The footage of my walk to the throne to take my royal position was played at every break during the two-and-a-half-day conference. Our full-body images in our dresses and crowns hung from the ceiling of the two-story lobby in front of the 4,000 seat auditorium. Smaller photos were posted on some of the doors leading into the church building and placed in frames on merchandise tables. My silhouette was printed on every ticket.

God went to great lengths to get this insecure girl's attention, but He got it.

In one way or another, God gets everyone's attention. I am not saying that He will do something as dramatic (or embarrassing) for you as He did for me, but I have a feeling that you could experience a surprising moment of revelation, too. There will be a day in the near future when the keys suddenly shine in your mind like a neon sign in the night.

Maybe you will be observing a man, speaking with a woman, watching boys or girls interacting in a park or a classroom, and it will all make sense. You will realize the door to healthy relationships has been unlocked, and you will want to share what you know because it could help them, too.

My heart is filled with the powerful stories people have shared with me over the last decade. I believe you will have some, too.

God stands ready to pour out the best of heaven when we accept our masculine and feminine identities and become who we were always meant to be.

FROM LEARNING TO LEGACY

And he will turn
The hearts of the fathers to the children,
And the hearts of the children to their fathers,
Lest I come and strike the earth with a curse."

Malachi 4:6 NKJV

You have come a long way! You've learned the keys to help you **Captivate, Cultivate, and Communicate** with both males and females of all ages. Now, the next move is yours. Will you begin to observe what's happening around you and ask God to give you the supernatural awareness and desire to activate what you've read and learned?

It's like putting on a new set of lenses that can bring a freedom you may not have experienced before. These principles are powerful, and they're yours when you choose to partner with the One who created us all from the beginning. I hope that excites you!

My lenses have been adjusting in this area for over a decade. The more I've learned, the more excited I become. But my heart also breaks for those who are trying so hard and still wondering, *"What is wrong?"* or *"How can I fix it?"*

Our lives may look different, but we all face the same road in the end. Eventually, each of us will leave this world and enter eternity. That reality brings two critical questions into focus:

1) Eternity is real—we're all heading toward it, either Heaven or Hell.

2) Legacy is inevitable—we all leave one, whether intentional or not.

Legacy follows us, good or bad. So what kind will it be for you? Many of us have faced the pain of harmful legacies. These are scars from a legacy we were born into and didn't create, choose, or deserve. Such legacies can cause regret and pain for generations. I hate, *yes hate, regrets.* We all have them, often due to ignorance, but we can choose not to carry them by responding differently the next time. I hope we keep a short list of deliberate acts of rebellion, selfish attitudes, and ambition.

As a relationship coach, I often help clients zoom out and gain a "bird's eye view" of how their decisions today will impact their future. Over a lifetime, we can look back and clearly see that repeating the same patterns, being stuck in destructive cycles, and ignoring warning signs eventually lead us to the same unwanted outcome. We can stay in a cycle for years without realizing there's a different way.

Instead of constantly focusing on what is visible—who is right or wrong, temporary gains, status, success, pain, moments of panic, or losing control— let's aim to see things from an eternal perspective.

Why does this matter?

When we learn to shift our focus beyond the present moment, we stop taking things so personally. It's not about us; it's about what God is doing in us for the sake of our legacy (and those we care about). We begin to see past roadblocks, confusion, pain, or the urgency of the moment and align our focus and responses with what will truly last. Most of the time, when I remember to do that, it brings balance, peace, and clarity into focus, pushing chaos and pain to the background. It's hard, but the Lord wants to help us. It's a good reminder that what is unseen is often far more valuable than what we can see. That is an invitation to activate our faith. We have the choice to believe that God is always at work, even when we don't fully understand, and it doesn't feel good.

For years, I watched myself and others around me deeply desiring to do right and "get it right." Unconsciously, we repeated the same cycles, trying to do what God was asking, but we didn't know how. My goal with this book was not to preach as if I have all the answers, but to share the things I have experienced and observed repeatedly through years of ministry.

1) We were committed, yet we struggled for over thirty years of marriage.

2) God was pursuing us and trying to help, but we couldn't see it.

3) I finally became lonely and frustrated enough to stop spinning and let the Lord speak.

4) When I humbled myself and chose to obey, He began the rescue.

5) It's never too late when people in relationships (of all kinds) choose to be teachable, vulnerable, and obedient.

The next step for you is to begin the activation process, looking at it from an eternal perspective for the sake of your legacy.

Many people associate the idea of legacy with tangible items of physical value. To me, it's not just about an inheritance; it's even more meaningful. It is a broader concept; legacy refers to what a person leaves behind emotionally, spiritually, culturally, or relationally. This also includes their values, reputation, and the impact they make on the world.

This is "why" it is important. This book offers keys to unlock the "how."

SOME EXAMPLES OF BUILDING A LEGACY ARE:

- How do I treat my spouse, children, or close friends, especially when no one is watching?

- Am I training my children with intention, even when it's inconvenient or hard?

- If you're married, in a serious relationship, or have children, is prayer together a part of your lives?

- Is my home a place of peace, joy, and safety for others?

- How do I respond when someone dishonors God, or when I do?

- What do I worship with my time, energy, and attention?

- Have I embraced my God-given male or female design and learned to walk in it with purpose?

Regardless of your relationship status—single, married, divorced, with or without kids—you are leaving a legacy. And it won't happen by chance. It requires focus, obedience, and a consistent partnership with God.

Believe God is good. He desires to position you and use you for His glory. He wants to grow and develop you, not just for your own benefit, but for the generations that follow.

So, what will you leave behind? How do you respond when life pushes back? What do your responses teach others?

Think about someone who valued you so intentionally—a grandparent, teacher, pastor, counselor, or coach—that they left a permanent impression on your heart. That's legacy. That's character. And that's what God is after in us.

Jesus died not just to forgive us but to give us His character. That's what will sustain us and give us true significance. This is demonstrated in how we live right now, in how we care for people and manage our relationships. That is what future generations will remember.

If you are willing, pray this prayer aloud over yourself:

"Lord, help me live today in light of eternity and build a legacy that reflects Your goodness and truth. In Jesus' name. Amen.

Prayer has power both now and for all eternity. When we pray, our words are held in the heart of the Father, even when they feel awkward or clunky to us. He honors our desire to connect with Him.

Many people don't grow up knowing how to pray, especially out loud. It's one of people's biggest fears. But when you speak to the King of the Universe, and someone else gets to listen, or you hear them do the same—it's powerful.

I was 36 before I really learned how to pray. Since then, I've discovered I wasn't alone. Because no one is born a prayer warrior, prayer must be taught or modeled. That's why I love the ACTS

Prayer model. It's simple, timeless, and has helped generations experience God's presence.

Use this tool. Share it. Let it build an emotional and spiritual connection between you, your friends, your family, and your Heavenly Father. Whether you're married, a parent, or single, it is for you.

A is for ADORATION

Focus your mind and heart on Whom you are speaking to: God, the Creator of everything, including you. You are entering into His presence.

It's helpful to change your physical position to get "there" faster.

Begin by stating aloud the character and attributes of the Father, Son, and the Holy Spirit. You may want to look in a concordance to find words that describe the attributes of God or pray a Psalm back to God.

C is for CONFESSION

Lay out what you may be struggling with, what you need help with, and where you feel weak. Include things that are tempting you or tripping you up, and things you have done (or continue to do) that you know hurt God's heart.

Tell Him you are sincerely sorry and ask for His forgiveness.

Ask Him to convict your heart so you can feel His Holy Spirit moving in your life and being. Remember, He will not use guilt.

T is for THANKSGIVING

Thank Him for specific things He has recently done for you, given to you, or spoken to you and those you care about.

Thank Him in advance for what you are "believing" for.

Thank Him for things He is revealing to you about Truth as you read and study His Word.

S is for SUPPLICATION

Ask Him for anything you need help with, things that are bigger than you, things that need His power, presence or attention.

Often, when we get to this portion, we are so full of gratitude it is hard to ask for anything more. However, if you have a need, He loves to hear from His kids specifically so He can answer, and you can readily recognize it was all His doing!

Be transparent and authentic. He knows your heart.

Remember the 'weed and the root' story from the introduction of this book? That story happened over thirty years ago, but it still speaks to us. Repositioning the eyes of our hearts can slowly change the way we think and respond. With an eternal perspective, our focus moves away from the present and toward a vision that includes those who will come after us.

As I write this conclusion, it is the day after the Fourth of July—Independence Day in the United States. The family Don and I began over four decades ago has grown. We now have two adult children, their wonderful spouses, and four grandchildren—two boys and two girls, ranging in age from one to seven and a half.

Yesterday, we all gathered in a circle around the kitchen to pray before our meal.

Don offered thanks for our nation and honored the brave men and women who have fought, and still fight, for our freedom. He also thanked the Lord for our family and for the parents and grandparents who came before us.

Typically, we ask the grandkids if anyone wants to pray, and they often volunteer. Let me assure you, Don and I didn't grow up in that kind of environment. We didn't know how to pray out loud. In my family, we recited memorized prayers. This is something new, something cultivated.

That day, the parents said, "This time Bubby wants to pray." After the prayer, they fixed the kids' plates and led them outside to eat at their small picnic table on the patio.

Then the adults came back in to serve their own plates.

As we were circling the island, our daughter-in-law Laura said, "Hey guys, look outside! The kids are praying!"

We all turned toward the window.

There they were: hands held, heads bowed, eyes closed—one by one, praying.

My 6'3" son-in-law, Jon, leaned over me, his voice barely a whisper, and his eyes filled with tears. "You should put this in your book."

He had no idea that this final chapter was about eternity and leaving a legacy.

Maybe you're reading this and thinking, "Good for you, but our family is too broken for that." Or, "It's too late for us." Or maybe you're wondering, "Where would we even start?"

Let me tell you:

It is never too late.

It only takes one person to begin turning the tide. One heart willing. One soul surrendered. With the right motive, belief in Jesus, and the Holy Spirit living in you to guide and teach—it is never too late.

Let the legacy begin with you.

DISCUSSION
QUESTIONS

Before we begin group
or pair discussions, please pause
and pray this prayer with me …

Lord,

As I hold this book in my hands, give me a teachable heart and the ability to absorb what You want to say to me. I may have beliefs that are shaping the way I think that are not aligned with You. If so, expose them! In some ways, this book may seem countercultural and the enemy, Satan, may try to bring confusion to keep me from pressing through to the end. Show me quickly when he is at work against what You want to do.

Show me any critical or cynical areas in me and replace them with Your wisdom. Help me surrender my soul (mind, will, and emotions) to what You want to do. If there are sections in this book that seem contrary to what I believe, pull me close and show me what You think about them. Lord, our culture seems confused, in pain, and full of fear. Sadly, the lies of the enemy have seeped into the Bride of Christ, and she is suffering. If You want to use this book to bring the genders back to Your original design, give me the desire and courage to read it and apply it to my life. Show me the lies about my gender and the opposite gender that may have been passed down for generations in my family. Infuse me with a clear understanding that "we are all products of our environment," but Jesus Christ reveals to heal and set us free.

Give me passion and courage as I walk through this journey with my heart and eyes wide open. Bring truth and transparency as You free me to become who You created me to be.

In the mighty name of Jesus, I pray,

Amen

 **CHAPTER 1 QUESTIONS**

How Two People Who Care About Each Other Can Drift Apart

Begin by reflecting on the following scripture after reading Chapter 1:

Let us not become weary in doing good, for at the proper time, we will reap a harvest if we do not give up.

(Galatians 6:9 NIV)

1. What's your relationship status? (Circle all that apply.)

    Single Dating   Recently Broken Up

    In a Relationship   Wish to Be Married

    In a Serious   Never wish to be

    Relationship Married   married Single Parent

    Separated   Married with Children

    Divorced   Other: _____

2. In one or two words, how would you describe the current condition of your heart? (Examples: free, loved, grateful, full, content, satisfied, lonely, hurting, rejected, abandoned, tired, exhausted, etc.)

    _____

    _____

_____

_____

_____

_____

_____

3. What's your personal goal for this book study?

    _____

    _____

    _____

    _____

    _____

    _____

    _____

4. There are usually one or two people of the opposite gender who
    stand out as extremely influential in your life, whether they be
    a spouse, parent, sibling, work colleague, or friend. Do you think
    you may have some misconceptions or unrealistic expectations
    of them? Where did those perspectives come from?

    _____

    _____

    _____

    _____

    _____

    _____

5. Do you think someone of the opposite gender may have misconceptions or unrealistic expectations of you? How is it affecting your relationship with that person?

_____

_____

_____

_____

_____

_____

6. Do you recognize any unhealthy attachments or entangled relationships in your life? These can be with anyone or anything that may have too much of your emotional attention and focus. These are people or things you focus on more than God. Check yourself by observing what captivates your mind during your waking hours. What is "the next right thing" the Lord may be asking you to do?

_____

_____

_____

_____

_____

_____

7. What does it mean to have a healthy "spiritual root system," and how are you developing yours? What are you doing to keep out the "weeds" in your relationships with God and others?

_____

_____

_____

_____

_____

_____

_____

8. What is your takeaway from this chapter—a special insight or practical step you plan to implement?

_____

_____

_____

_____

_____

_____

_____

 **CHAPTER 2 QUESTIONS**

What's Happened to Our Hearts?

Begin by reflecting on the following scripture after reading Chapter 2:

We know that we are children of God, and that the whole world is under the control of the evil one.

(1 John 5:19 NIV)

1. From your observation, what does our current culture suggest about both genders? If possible, give examples.

    _____

    _____

    _____

    _____

    _____

    _____

    _____

2. What is your opinion of each gender, based on your personal interactions?

    _____

    _____

_____

3. Do you believe God's original design was to make males and females different? If so, why?

_____

4. Do you think you fit into some of society's stereotypes of your gender? How has that affected you?

_____

5. What do you think God sees and feels about you when He looks at you?

_____

_____

_____

_____

_____

_____

6. Do you believe God's desire is to reveal, heal, and restore you to His design and plan? What is your initial reaction to this idea?

_____

_____

_____

_____

_____

_____

7. What could life look like if we were living in a world where men appreciated the unique qualities of women, and women appreciated the unique qualities of men?

_____

_____

_____

_____

_____

_____

_____

8. What is your takeaway from this chapter—a special insight or practical step you plan to implement?

    _____

    _____

    _____

    _____

    _____

    _____

 **CHAPTER 3 QUESTIONS**

Different by Design

Begin by reflecting on the following scripture after reading Chapter 3:

The world is unprincipled. It's dog-eat-dog out there! The world doesn't fight fair. But we don't live or fight our battles that way—never have and never will. The tools of our trade aren't for marketing or manipulation, but they are for demolishing that entire massively corrupt culture. We use our powerful God-tools for smashing warped philosophies, tearing down barriers erected against the truth of God, fitting every loose thought and emotion and impulse into the structure of life shaped by Christ. Our tools are ready at hand for clearing the ground of every obstruction and building lives of obedience into maturity.

(2 Corinthians 10:3-6 MSG)

1. Think about the process of building a house, office, organization, department, team, ministry, business, family, etc. Consider what both genders generally bring to the project. What might be the downside to building anything without …

Women:

_____

_____

_____

_____

_____

_____

Men:

_____

_____

_____

_____

_____

_____

2. What evidence have you seen that confirms there is still a little boy or little girl inside each of us, regardless of our age?

_____

_____

_____

_____

_____

_____

3. In your opinion, what is God's motive for commanding that His children submit to one another?

_____

_____

_____

_____

_____

_____

4. Is there someone in your life who has modeled healthy godly submission to authority? What did you learn from what you observed?

_____

_____

_____

_____

_____

_____

5. When you read over the differences between men and women, what stood out or made sense to you in a new way?

_____

_____

_____

_____

_____

_____

_____

6. Do you believe God sees and understands the deep desires
    of your heart, just like He did for Adam? How do you know?

    _____

    _____

    _____

    _____

    _____

    _____

    _____

7. In what ways are the specific differences of the opposite gen-
    der God's answer to your desires? In what ways can your
    specific gender differences be an answer for someone else?

    _____

    _____

    _____

    _____

    _____

    _____

8. What is your takeaway from this chapter—a special insight or practical step you plan to implement?

    _____

    _____

    _____

    _____

    _____

    _____

    _____

 **CHAPTER 4 QUESTIONS**

Different for a Purpose

Begin by reflecting on the following scripture after reading Chapter 4:

And the glory which You gave Me I have given them, that they may be one just as We are one: I in them, and You in Me; that they may be made perfect in one, and that the world may know that You have sent Me, and have loved them as You have loved Me.

(John 17:22-23 NKJV)

1. Make a list of the women and men who have played an important role in your life.

_____

_____

_____

_____

_____

_____

_____

2. After you have written down the names, write out the positive attributes you see in them.

_____

_____

_____

_____

_____

_____

_____

3. How do you think these men and women see themselves? Do you think they are aware of their inner beauty? Why or why not?

_____

_____

_____

_____

_____

_____

_____

4. How do you think God sees them?

_____

_____

_____

_____

_____

_____

_____

5. What can you do to help them see their worth and value to God and step up and into the position God created for them?

_____

_____

_____

_____

_____

_____

6. Ask the Lord to show you how He sees them and how you can affirm their God-given purpose.

_____

_____

_____

_____

_____

_____

7. What is your takeaway from this chapter—a special insight or practical step you plan to implement?

 **CHAPTER 5 QUESTIONS**

Key #1 For Men: Captivate

Begin by reflecting on the following scripture after reading Chapter 5:

What you say goes, God, and stays, as permanent as the heavens. Your truth never goes out of fashion; it's as relevant as the earth when the sun comes up. Your Word and truth are dependable as ever; that's what you ordered—you set the earth going. If your revelation hadn't delighted me so, I would have given up when the hard times came. But I'll never forget the advice you gave me; you saved my life with those wise words. Save me! I'm all yours. I look high and low for your words of wisdom. The wicked lie in ambush to destroy me, but I'm only concerned with your plans for me. I see the limits to everything human, but the horizons can't contain your commands!

(Psalm 119:89-96 MSG)

1. How does it feel to interact with a man who has humility, authority, and honor? How does this behavior affect the way you view or relate to him?

_____

_____

_____

_____

_____

_____

_____

2. What does the term "code of honor" mean to you? How would you describe it to someone who had never heard it?

_____

_____

_____

_____

_____

_____

_____

3. Where have you witnessed a man thriving as part of a team?

_____

_____

_____

_____

_____

_____

_____

4. If your family of origin displayed male roles according to God's design, take a moment to share your experience.

    _____

    _____

    _____

    _____

    _____

    _____

    _____

5. If your family of origin did not display male roles according to God's design, take a moment to forgive.

    _____

    _____

    _____

    _____

    _____

    _____

    _____

6. Do you know a single man—whether with children or without—who exhibits what it means to be masculine and strong, even though he may need to operate in the role of nurturer? What is he doing well?

    _____

    _____

_____

_____

_____

_____

_____

7. Do you know a woman who captivates men? Describe what makes her stand out as an example to you. (You can choose someone you know personally or someone you have observed from afar.)

_____

_____

_____

_____

_____

_____

_____

8. What is your takeaway from this chapter—a special insight or practical step you plan to implement?

_____

_____

_____

_____

_____

_____

 **CHAPTER 6 QUESTIONS**

Key #2 For Men: Cultivate

Begin by reflecting on the following scripture after reading Chapter 6:

Be patient, therefore, brothers,[a] until the coming of the Lord. See how the farmer waits for the precious fruit of the earth, being patient about it, until it receives the early and the late rains. 8 You also, be patient. Establish your hearts, for the coming of the Lord is at hand.

(James 5:7-8 ESV)

1. Have you ever observed a man create a personal routine to honor his need for transition time (whether or not he is aware that is what he is doing)? Describe what it looked like.

_____

_____

_____

_____

_____

_____

2. Men, what would be possible for you if people intentionally cultivated your masculine identity by giving you space to try new things?

    _____

    _____

    _____

    _____

    _____

    _____

3. What are a few unique hobbies or physical outlets you have seen men enjoy?

    _____

    _____

    _____

    _____

    _____

    _____

4. Men, share a memory of a time when you felt truly success-ful and that your effort to achieve a goal for your team was worth it.

    _____

    _____

---

5. Have you ever experienced a "shoulder-to-shoulder" situation with a man for work or play? What did you notice about the experience?

---

6. Can you think of a man who is an excellent example of some-one who leads without dominating? What is he like? (You can choose someone you know personally or someone you have observed from afar.)

_____

_____

7. In what ways has the Lord been cultivating you recently?

_____

_____

_____

_____

_____

_____

8. What is your takeaway from this chapter—a special insight or practical step you plan to implement?

_____

_____

_____

_____

_____

_____

 **CHAPTER 7 QUESTIONS**

Key #3 For Men: Communicate

Begin by reflecting on the following scripture after reading Chapter 7:

The words of the reckless pierce like swords, but the tongue of the wise brings healing.

(Proverbs 12:18 NIV)

1. Men, how does it feel to communicate with people who honor you by verbalizing appreciation for who you are and what you do? How does this behavior affect the way you view or relate to them?

_____

_____

_____

_____

_____

_____

_____

2. What is it like to interact specifically with a woman who comes across as independent, self-sufficient, or self-righteous? What about a woman who never asks for or accepts your assistance?

3. How does it feel to communicate with a man who comes across as demanding, entitled, or controlling? What about a man who is disengaged and passive?

4. In this chapter, you were given a step-by-step outline for inviting conversation with a man. Men, how would you respond to an invitation like this?

---

5. Do you know a man who takes time to think (more time than feels comfortable for you) before answering a question? How can that tendency produce positive results?

---

6. Men, please explain how you take it when someone interrupts you. What does it imply about the other person?

---

7. Men, why does it help to know the bullet points—or bottom line—before a conversation begins?

---

8. What is your takeaway from this chapter—a special insight or practical step you plan to implement?

 **CHAPTER 8 QUESTIONS**

Key #1 For Women: Captivate

Begin by reflecting on the following scripture after reading Chapter 8:

A good woman is hard to find, and worth far more than dia-monds. Her husband trusts her without reserve, and never has reason to regret it. Never spiteful, she treats him gen-erously all her life long ... Charm can mislead and beauty soon fades. The woman to be admired and praised is the woman who lives in the Fear-of-God. Give her everything she deserves! Adorn her life with praises!

(Proverbs 31:10-12, 30-31 MSG)

1. How does it feel to be with a woman who speaks life, submits, and creates warm and welcoming environments? How does this behavior affect the way you view or relate to her?

    _____

    _____

    _____

    _____

    _____

2. Women, think back on the last 48 hours, where were the moments when your fear factor was on alert and you felt unsafe?

_____

_____

_____

_____

_____

_____

3. If your family of origin displayed female roles according to God's design, take a moment to share your experience.

_____

_____

_____

_____

_____

_____

4. If your family of origin did not display female roles according to God's design, take a moment to forgive.

_____

_____

_____

_____

_____

_____

_____

5. Do you know a single woman—whether with children or with-
    out—who exhibits what it means to be feminine and heart-
    strong, even though she operates in the role of provider? What
    is she doing well?

_____

_____

_____

_____

_____

_____

6. Have you ever observed a man of any age who captivates
    women? Describe him. What makes him stand out as an exam-
    ple to you? (You can choose someone you know personally or
    someone you have observed from afar).

_____

_____

_____

_____

_____

7. What does the term "hero" mean to you? How would you explain the type of hero a woman is always looking for?

8. What is your takeaway from this chapter—a special insight or practical step you plan to implement?

 **CHAPTER 9 QUESTIONS**

Key #2 For Women: Cultivate

Begin by reflecting on the following scripture after reading Chapter 9:

And if you will indeed obey my commandments that I command you today, to love the Lord your God, and to serve him with all your heart and with all your soul, 14 he[a] will give the rain for your land in its season, the early rain and the later rain, that you may gather in your grain and your wine and your oil. 15 And he will give grass in your fields for your livestock, and you shall eat and be full.

(Deuteronomy 11:13-15 ESV)

1. Women, what would be possible for you if people intentionally cultivated your feminine identity?

_____

_____

_____

_____

_____

_____

_____

2. Have you ever observed a woman create a personal routine to honor her need to beautify environments (whether or not she is aware that is what she is doing)? Describe what it looked like.

_____

_____

_____

_____

_____

_____

_____

3. Describe a time when you witnessed a female exhibiting her adaptability.

_____

_____

_____

_____

_____

_____

_____

4. Think of how a scenario without women could have negatively affected you throughout your lifetime? Explain.

_____

_____

----

5. Women, which aspects of your environment speak loudest to you and are most difficult to ignore? How can others in your family and workplace help you in this area?

----

6. What can emotionally healthy girlfriends give to each other that a man cannot?

----

7. As an interesting experiment, ask the women in the group to share what is on their radar system right now.

_____

_____

_____

_____

_____

_____

8. What is your takeaway from this chapter—a special insight or practical step you plan to implement?

_____

_____

_____

_____

_____

_____

 **CHAPTER 10 QUESTIONS**

Key #3 For Women: Communicate

Begin by reflecting on the following scripture after reading Chapter 10:

He who answers a matter before he hears it, it is folly and shame to him.

(Proverbs 18:13 NKJV)

1. Women, how does it feel to communicate with people who care for you by taking time for meaningful conversations? How does this behavior affect the way you view or relate to them?

_____

_____

_____

_____

_____

_____

2. Women, what is it like to interact with a man who makes decisions that could affect you but does not communicate or consider your opinion?

_____

_____

_____

_____

_____

_____

3. Describe how it feels when you are communicating with a woman who comes across as harsh, manipulative, or critical. What about a woman who is silent and passive?

_____

_____

_____

_____

_____

_____

4. What can you do to provide safety and reassurance the next time you see a woman "overtalking?"

_____

_____

_____

_____

_____

_____

_____

5. Have you seen or heard a female of any age express her emo-
    tions physically, such as with gasps, groans, hand movements,
    or animated facial expressions? Share an example.

    _____

    _____

    _____

    _____

    _____

    _____

6. Ladies, knowing how you are wired for emotional connection, is
    there a single friend you could reach out to this week—to listen
    and offer her the kind of support only a safe, caring friend can
    give? (Men, a word of caution: when a woman is in a vulnerable
    emotional state, connection—even when well-intended—can
    easily be misunderstood. Unless you have a clearly defined
    relationship with her, it's usually not wise or honoring to step
    into that role. Boundaries matter for both of you.)

    _____

    _____

    _____

----

7. Women, please describe some examples of non-sexual touch from your husbands or boyfriends that are meaningful to you. Can you also share an example of a platonic, helpful touch from friends or people who desire to help or serve you?

----

8. What is your takeaway from this chapter—a special insight or practical step you plan to implement?

 **CHAPTER 11 QUESTIONS**

In Need of Rescue

Begin by reflecting on the following scripture after reading Chapter 11:

And let us spur one another on toward love and good deeds, not giving up meeting together, as some are in the habit of doing, but encouraging one another—and all the more, as you see the Day approaching.

(Hebrews 10:24-25 NIV)

1. With God, nothing is over until He says it is over. How have you seen that proven true in your own life? How does knowing this encourage you?

_____

_____

_____

_____

_____

_____

_____

2. In what ways have you experienced opposition from the enemy since you began this book study?

3. What changes have you noticed in yourself since you began this book study?

4. What changes have you noticed about how the opposite gender responds to you since you began implementing the keys?

_____

_____

_____

5. What have you done in the past when you sense that you are slipping into old habits you desire to leave behind? What, if anything, can you commit to do differently when that happens in the future?

_____

_____

_____

_____

_____

_____

_____

6. What have you done in the past when you sense that a person you love is slipping into old habits you thought they had left behind? What, if anything, can you commit to do differently when that happens in the future?

_____

_____

_____

_____

_____

_____

7. Have you noticed a friend or relative who needs freedom and healing in their relationships with the opposite gender? How can you encourage them? What do you think would happen if you shared this book with them?

_____

_____

_____

_____

_____

_____

_____

8. What is your takeaway from this chapter—a special insight or practical step you plan to implement?

_____

_____

_____

_____

_____

_____

_____

 **CHAPTER 12 QUESTIONS**

In Position for Reset

Begin by reflecting on the following scripture after reading Chapter 12:

Even when I am old and gray, do not forsake me, my God, till I declare your power to the next generation, your mighty acts to all who are to come. Your righteousness, God, reaches to the heavens, you who have done great things. Who is like you, God? Though you have made me see troubles, many and bitter, you will restore my life again; from the depths of the earth, you will again bring me up. You will increase my honor and comfort me once more.

(Psalm 71:18-21 NIV)

1. What do you imagine would be possible in your family and workplace if males and females walked in their true identities?

_____

_____

_____

_____

_____

_____

_____

2. How would the church look different if everyone freely operated from God-given their masculinity and femininity?

3. Have you ever seen evidence of godly plans being aborted because males or females were not operating according to their divine design? Explain.

4. In this chapter, you read, "Spiritually speaking, the church should not be trying to do what only God can do, and God should not have to do what the church should be doing." What should the church be doing? What kinds of things can only God do?

------

5. Has there been a time when God went to great lengths to get your attention? What happened?

------

6. If you could share a few concepts from the keys with the next generation, how would you explain them in a simple way that could prepare young people for their future without sounding preachy?

------

7. Now that you know the profound benefits of the keys, are there a few people you would like to thank? Has a male or female been interacting with you according to these principles, without realizing it? Who can you encourage for displaying even one of these concepts?

_____

_____

_____

_____

_____

_____

_____

8. What is your takeaway from this chapter—a special insight or practical step you plan to implement?

_____

_____

_____

_____

_____

_____

_____

 **CHAPTER 13 QUESTIONS**

From Learning to Legacy

Begin by reflecting on the following scripture after reading Chapter 13:

One generation shall commend your works to another, and shall declare your mighty acts.

(Psalm 145:4 ESV)

1. What kind of legacy have you received from those who went before you? Be as specific as you can.

_____

_____

_____

_____

_____

_____

2. What kind of legacy would you like to leave for those who come after you? Be specific.

_____

_____

_____

_____

_____

_____

_____

3. Are you comfortable praying aloud? If so, who taught you to pray by modeling it? If no one has, do you desire to learn? If prayer is talking to the ONE who loves you most, what are you afraid of?

_____

_____

_____

_____

_____

_____

4. Imagine an ideal scene in the future where children demonstrate an understanding of the concepts you've learned and are applying from this book. What would look different from what you typically see among children today?

_____

_____

_____

_____

_____

_____

_____

5. Everyone hears the voice of God in different ways. Have you heard the Lord speak to you during this study? What did you hear, and what was that experience like?

_____

_____

_____

_____

_____

_____

6. Off the top of your head, name the one key for men or women that has been most helpful or produced the most transformation in you during this book study.

_____

_____

_____

_____

_____

_____

7. What have you gained from this experience? How do you plan to apply the keys to your life, and how might this affect your legacy in a positive way, possibly breaking a cycle that was handed down to you?

_____

_____

_____

_____

_____

_____

8. Over the past decade, many readers have shared that these keys are something they need to revisit year after year, because our culture is so different from the keys. How do you feel about that? Could this become part of your yearly rhythm—a time to refocus, realign, and remind yourself who God says you are and how He's equipped you to live?

_____

_____

_____

_____

_____

_____

ACKNOWLEDGMENTS

To Don, thank you for partnering with God to provide for and protect our family and me. My life and my relationship with you are more than I ever dreamed or imagined. Thank you for not giving up on us or me. Thank you for never ceasing to war for us—no matter what came against you.

To our children – Jonathan and Holly – You are both so much more than we could have ever imagined when we dreamed of having children, all of those years ago. Thank you for following the Lord in your lives and for allowing Him to guide you in choosing your spouses. We are deeply grateful for how beautifully Jon and Laura fit into our now-family of ten. We couldn't have written a better story ourselves, nor would we have wanted to.

To our grandchildren—Merrick, Decklan, Kenley, and Hazel.

ABOUT THE AUTHOR

Cristie Penn has been teaching, facilitating groups, and mentoring leaders for more than three decades. As a certified John Maxwell Coach, speaker, and relationship coach, she has shared biblical truth at conferences, churches, and retreats across the U.S. and abroad. Cristie is the confidant who sits across the table with a biblical perspective, a story to tell, and a heart that listens and cares. Drawing from both personal experience and years of ministry, she helps others see themselves the way God designed them. She and her husband Don live in Southlake, Texas, where they enjoy life with their married children, their spouses, and four precious grandchildren.

NOTES

www.ingramcontent.com/pod-product-compliance
Lightning Source LLC
Chambersburg PA
CBHW060134130626
46556CB00006B/2344